AF477991

SCIENCE FICTION
AND FANTASY

Our Freedom to Read

Coming-of-Age Fiction

Outsider Fiction

Classic Books

Science Fiction and Fantasy

SCIENCE FICTION
AND FANTASY

STEVEN OTFINOSKI

Library of Congress Cataloging-in-Publication Data
Otfinoski, Steven.
Our freedom to read / Steven Otfinoski.
v. cm.
Includes bibliographical references and indexes.
Contents: [1] Classic books — [2] Coming-of-age fiction —
[3] Outsider fiction — [4] Science fiction and fantasy.
ISBN 978-1-60413-029-4 (v. 1 : acid-free paper) — ISBN 978-1-60413-030-0
(v. 2 : acid-free paper) — ISBN 978-1-60413-031-7 (v. 3 : acid-free paper) —
ISBN 978-1-60413-032-4 (v. 4 : acid-free paper)
1. Prohibited books—Bibliography—Juvenile literature. 2. Challenged books—Bibliography—
Juvenile literature. 3. Expurgated books—Bibliography—Juvenile literature. 4. Prohibited
books—United States—Bibliography—Juvenile literature. 5. Challenged books—United States—
Bibliography—Juvenile literature. 6. Expurgated books—United States—Bibliography—Juvenile
literature. 7. Children's stories—Censorship—United States—Case studies—Juvenile literature.
8. Young adult fiction—Censorship—United States—Case studies—Juvenile literature.
9. Children's stories—Bio-bibliography—Juvenile literature. 10. Young adult fiction—
Bio-bibliography—Juvenile literature. I. Title.
Z1019.O84 2009
098'.1—dc22
2008032030

Contents

Introduction

Some of the most popular books for children and young adults fall into the categories of science fiction, fantasy, and horror. Book series such as *Harry Potter, Goosebumps, Scary Stories, Captain Underpants,* and *His Dark Materials* have sold in the millions. Dark, macabre stories and poems have made Roald Dahl and Shel Silverstein best-selling authors. Ray Bradbury and Stephen King have been hailed as the reigning champs of, respectively, science fiction/fantasy and horror for both young readers and adults. The opportunity to enter another world filled with adventure and imagination is irresistible to young readers, who often devour such books as quickly as they can get their hands on them.

Science fiction (sci-fi) deals with some aspect of science and technology and is often set in the future. The sci-fi titles considered here deal with the future, one that is particularly grim. They fit into the subgenre of dystopia, depicting future societies that are unpleasant and twisted, where the individual is repressed and controlled. These books are the exact opposite of utopian novels, which reveal a happy future for humankind. *Brave New World* and *The Giver* present worlds where love and passion have been largely erased, only to be replaced by comfort and stability. In *Fahrenheit 451,* books are banned for spreading "dangerous" ideas, while in *A Wrinkle in Time* and the *His Dark Materials* trilogy, science, religion, and technology are used to control people's minds and actions. The protagonists in all of these books, three of them children, manage to escape from the destructive society that threatens them, by finding a safe haven with other like-minded people or destroying the forces of evil, or, as in the case of John Savage in *Brave New World,* through death.

Fantasy shares some similarities with science fiction, but it deals with very different imaginative worlds—worlds where animals and insects can talk (*James and the Giant Peach*), children can fly in airplanes made of batter (*In the Night Kitchen*), families live silly and outrageous lives (*The Stupids*), and ordinary people possess extraordinary powers (*Captain Underpants*).

Horror involves the supernatural, too, but in ways meant to fill readers more with fear than wonder. Horror is populated with ghosts (*Scary Stories*), witches (*The Witches*), werewolves (*Blood and Chocolate*), and everyday horrors, like a rabid dog that kills its master (*Cujo*).

Although the majority of the titles covered here are novels and picture books, this volume also discusses poetry (*Witches, Witches, Witches*; *Halloween ABC*; and *A Light in the Attic*), graphic novels (*Captain Underpants*), and narrative nonfiction (*Curses, Hexes & Spells*).

Science fiction, fantasy, and horror books are among the most popular in modern children's literature, but they are also—in the eyes of some parents, teachers, and school administrators—among the most controversial. Thirteen of the books discussed in this volume made the American Library Association's "100 Most Frequently Challenged Books of 1990–2000." Four of these landed in the top twenty titles, with Alvin Schwartz's *Scary Stories* series having the dubious honor of first place.

What is it about this kind of literature that makes censors and challengers see red? Where young readers see wonder and magic, some adults see satanic powers at work. Perhaps author Judy Blume, who does not write fantasy fiction, put it best when she wrote: "Today it is not only Sex, Swear Words, and Lack of Moral Tone—it is Evil, which according to the censors, can be found lurking everywhere. Stories about Halloween, witches, and devils are all suspect for promoting Satanism . . . Madeleine L'Engle's *A Wrinkle in Time*, for promoting New Age-ism . . . There's not an *ism* you can think of that's not bringing some book to the battlefield."

That battlefield is littered with banned books, successful challenges, and wounded readers. At times the war against fantasy literature, as most dramatically seen in the attacks on the *Harry Potter* books by many fundamentalist Christian groups, resembles a New England witch hunt more than 300 years ago. Some adults link fantasy to witchcraft and witchcraft to supposedly destructive feminist practices. "The feminist agenda is not about equal rights for women," declared far-right Christian leader Pat Robertson. "It is about a socialist, anti-family political movement that encourages women to leave their husbands, kill their children, practice witchcraft, and become lesbians." Many less political challengers still believe the agenda of writers like J. K. Rowling and Philip Pullman is to transform innocent children into occult-practicing wizards, witches, and warlocks.

Whereas witchcraft in these books may be accused of seducing the young, horror is usually seen as scaring the wits out of them. Many parents fear that the ghastly doings in *Goosebumps*, *Scary Stories*, and other young-adult horror series can leave traumatic, psychic scars on children. Although a few challenges have pointed to children having nightmares after reading one of these books, the majority of children who read them delight in the gruesome goings-on. Like many adults who read Stephen King novels and watch horror movies, they enjoy the pleasure of being scared.

The horrors of *Blood and Chocolate*, a contemporary novel about teen werewolves, strike closer to home. Some critics have seen the monsters in this and other novels as symbols for the alienation that most young people experience at one time or another. Stephen King is adept at conjuring up all sorts of ghosts and monsters from his active imagination, but in *Cujo* the monster is the friendly Saint Bernard down the street who one day is bitten on the nose by a rabid bat. The horrors of *Cujo* are all to real, and that may explain why of all King's bloody works, it is the one most frequently challenged in schools.

For Stephen King, however, censorship itself is "a scary idea." In a 1989 interview, he had this advice for students: "Whatever it is that your parents and teachers don't want you to read is probably the thing that you need the most to find out. So I would find out what's being censored, what's been pulled from the shelves of your school library, and I would *run* to the nearest public library or to a bookstore and pick it up . . . . "

Kids are picking up fantasy literature and devouring it. While parents may shudder at the wacky horrors of *Goosebumps* or the gross-out, bathroom humor that infuses every *Captain Underpants* book, they can take some solace in the fact that these books are getting their children to read, exercise their imaginations, and develop a true love of literature. And that may not be so wicked after all.

Challenges, Censorship, and This Book

What exactly is a challenge to a book? The American Library Association (ALA), founded in 1876, monitors challenges and defines a book challenge as a "formal, written complaint filed with a library or school requesting that materials be removed because of content or appropriateness." According to the ALA, there were 546 book challenges in 2006, an increase of thirty percent from 2005. The organization considers that number in "the mid-range" and rather low compared to the peak years of the mid-1990s, when book challenges numbered more than 750 annually. Some experts attribute the surge at that time to the appearance of the *Harry Potter* series, one of the most challenged book series of all time.

Why does the ALA care about these challenges and monitor them so closely? "One of the things we believe is that materials need to be available to people so that they can make their own choices," former associate director of the ALA's Office for Intellectual Freedom Cynthia Robinson said. "Removing books suppresses that point of view . . . . The First Amendment is very important to librarians and one of our most important rights as Americans. It's so fundamental I think people often take it for granted . . . supporting intellectual freedom [and] the right of individuals and their families to decide what they're going to read is one of the association's most important missions and by far one of its most public."

Most book challenges noted by the ALA are made initially by parents of students who become aware of a book's content when their child brings it home to read or study. In many cases, these challengers reject the honest depiction of the real world—and the language and behavior of those who inhabit it. Some adults do not care for their children to know what life is like in the netherworld of the drug addict or behind the locked gates of a boys' reformatory or a psychiatric hospital. Other challenges arise over the very issues that the authors are challenging and criticizing, such as physical or sexual child abuse, racism, and bullying in schools. Still other critics resent the proposition put forth in a number of these books that it is largely the system—whether school administrators, misguided parents, or corrupt governments—that is to blame for the injustices depicted.

They are disturbed by the authors' sharp criticism of authority in all its forms.

When a formal challenge is made, the school district takes it seriously. In most cases, the school board or school superintendent will turn the matter over to a special review committee for consideration. The committee may already be established, but in many cases it may only be formed when needed. The committee members may include school administrators, media specialists, teachers, parents, area residents, and even students. The challenged book may continue to remain in use in the school or in circulation in the school library while the committee is deliberating, although in some cases the book is removed during this period.

After reading the challenged book, possibly hearing more from the challengers, and discussing the matter among themselves, the committee members come up with a recommendation that is passed on to the school board. The school board then meets to consider the recommendation and votes to either accept the recommendation as it is or make another decision about the challenged book. Sometimes the school superintendent will play an important role in this decision.

Many challenges are rejected. According to Judith Krug, director of ALA's Office for Intellectual Freedom, only thirty out of the 546 challenged books were actually banned in 2006. These bans can take several forms. Some result in the complete removal of a book from the classroom and school library. In other cases, the book is taken from the classroom but is retained on the school library shelves, sometimes with limited access to certain grades or to be borrowed only with written parental permission. In still other cases, the challenged book is removed from one grade but taught in a higher grade where it is considered more appropriate.

Some book challenges are questionable or even absurd. In one case, parents in McKinleyville, California, challenged the joke book, *Laugh Lines*, in 1990 and wanted it removed from the elementary school library. The challenge claimed it was "demeaning" toward readers who read the riddles and couldn't come up with the correct answers. Other challenges are trivial. One parent, noted in a "Landmark Challenge" in this series, complained about the single use of a swear word by a character in a novel. Some challenges are misguided. According to the ALA, the most challenged book in both 2006 and

2007 was the children's picture book, *And Tango Makes Three*, the true story of two male penguins that raise a baby penguin without a female. Parents complained that the book promoted a homosexual lifestyle. The same book was praised by the ALA as one of the best picture books of 2006.

"So many adults are exhausting themselves worrying about other people corrupting their children with books, they're turning kids off to reading instead of turning them on," wrote Judy Blume in the introduction to a collection of stories by banned writers. "In this age of censorship I mourn the loss of books that will never be written, I mourn the voices that will be silenced—writers' voices, teachers' voices, students' voices—and all because of fear."

The most important part of this volume is not the description of the challenges themselves but of the courageous voices that rose up in opposition to support and defend these books. In many cases, they made the difference—ending a challenge or bringing a banned book back into the classroom or back on to the library shelf. These books are a cry for tolerance and justice in our world. They stand up for diversity and the differences that make us each unique individuals. If we deny ourselves their wisdom, wit, and power, we will all end up as the ultimate losers—estranged from one another, society, and ourselves.

The format of this book is straightforward. Each entry covers a single banned or challenged book, presented in chronological order by date of publication. Entries start with a brief, concise summary of the book in the "What Happens in" section. This is followed by "Challenges and Censorship," which may include some or all of the following: the history of how the author came to write the book, its initial reception from reviewers and readers, and the main reasons why it has been challenged in schools. Next is one or more "Landmark Challenges" described in detail. Some landmark challenges include several related challenges. Finally, each entry concludes with a list of sources for "Further Reading" and a brief biography of the author or authors in "About the Author of."

Why a series about book banning? Can we learn something from these cases of challenges and censorship of fiction? The American Library Association thinks so, which is why it reports on challenges from around the nation and the world in its monthly *Newsletter on Intellectual Freedom*, a publication now more than a half century old. The ALA also sponsors Banned Books Week each year to focus attention on books that have been banned.

"Throughout history, there always have been a few people who don't want information to be freely available. And this is still true," said ALA president Leslie Burger during Banned Books Week 2006. "The reason more books aren't banned is because community residents—with librarians, teachers, and journalists—stand up and speak out for their freedom to read." As long as we all recognize censorship when it arises and speak out against it, that freedom will remain secure.

Brave New World (1932)
by Aldous Huxley

What Happens in *Brave New World*

The time is the not-so-distant future, when society on earth has finally abolished war and established universal peace. But this peace comes at a high price. Love among individuals has also been abolished. There are no traditional families, and people go freely from one sexual relationship to another. Each individual is genetically engineered and produced through incubation, not from a mother's womb. The only emotion and loyalty an individual has is to the state, which controls every aspect of life. Once a person reaches the age of sixty, he or she is given an overdose of the universal drug *soma*. Then the corpse is burned and used as fertilizer.

A small minority of people, called "savages," continues to live in the traditions of the past in isolated regions. One of these regions is in the southwestern United States, where social misfit Bernard Marx takes his new girlfriend, Lenina Crowne, on a vacation. There they meet John, a young white man who has been raised among Native Americans by his mother, Linda, who was stranded there years earlier. Bernard and Lenina are quite taken with John and bring him and Linda back with them to civilization. Linda, overweight and shunned by others, is put into a hospital where she spends her last days on a continual soma high, while her son becomes a celebrity of sorts to the smart people of this "brave new world."

John falls hopelessly in love with Lenina, but quickly realizes that her interest in him is superficial and that she, like the others, cannot experience love. When he disrupts the distribution of soma, John is brought, with Bernard, before the Controller. This authority figure understands John's longing for the "old ways" and its culture, but he sums up the rationale behind the new order in a speech: "People are happy; they get what they want, and they never want what they can't get. They're well off; they're safe; they're never ill; they're not afraid of death; they're blissfully ignorant of passion and old age; they're plagued with no mothers or fathers; they've got no wives, or children, or lovers to feel strongly about; they're so conditioned that they practically can't help behaving as they ought to behave. And if anything should go wrong, there's soma."

Unable to deal any longer with the civilization he hoped would fulfill him, John flees the city and attempts to recreate his old Native life—living off the land. But even here reporters and curiosity seekers hound him. In despair, he finally hangs himself.

Challenges and Censorship

Brave New World was not well received on its publication in England on February 2, 1932. Most critics and reviewers found it shallow and one-note in its satire. "A lugubrious and heavy-handed piece of propaganda," wrote M. C. Dawson in the journal *Books*. The conservative Catholic Board of Censors of Ireland banned the book in that country, calling it "depressing, fatalistic, and negative." One of the few positive reviews was by Edward Cushing, who wrote in the *Saturday Review of Literature*: "Mr. Huxley is elegant in his declaration of an artist's faith in man, and it is his eloquence, bitter in attack, noble in defense, that when one has closed his book, one remembers . . . ."

Despite its tepid reception among the press, *Brave New World* was a reasonably good seller. It sold 13,000 copies its first year in England and another 10,000 the following year. It was not as popular initially in the United States, selling fewer than 3,000 copies on its initial publication.

In the decades since Huxley's death, the novel has been included on many high school reading lists for its condemnation of a materialistic and hedonistic society. But its use in classrooms has led to numerous challenges. The novel ranked fifty-second on the American Library Association's "100 Most Frequently Challenged Books of 1990–2000." Most challenges have focused on references to drug use, sex, and conformity, as well as the final suicide of the protagonist, John Savage.

Huxley himself hoped his novel would make people think about the world's future before it was too late. "We are getting more and more into a position where these things can be achieved," he said in a 1961 interview. "And it's extremely important to realize this, and to take every possible precaution to see that they shall not be achieved. This, I take it was the message of the book—*This is possible: for heaven's sake be careful about it.*"

Landmark Challenge:
Taking on the Law in Gallatin

An obscenity law in Tennessee that made it a misdemeanor to provide sexually explicit or violent materials to minors caused a stir over *Brave New World* and other classic novels in Sumner County schools in 1997.

That fall, the mother of a Beech High School student in Gallatin complained when her daughter was assigned to read the Huxley novel as well as *Catch-22*, by Joseph Heller. While the challenge did not lead to the books' banning, it caused some concern to the school's director, Merrol Hyde. In an interview in early January 1998, Hyde told the press that he questioned the wisdom of the school district's putting these two novels and other books with adult content on assigned reading lists when they could be breaking the state obscenity law.

A few days later, the school board countered the director's words. "We're not in here this evening to ban any books," declared board member Billy Hobbs, a former school principal. "We're not here to have any book bannings or censorship. This whole thing has been blown out of proportion."

While assuring the public neither book would be removed from schools, the board voted unanimously to incorporate the obscenity law into official school board policy.

Landmark Challenge:
Too Brave in Alabama

"You would not believe what they're having us read in English class," a friend of Kathleen Stone's child told her in 2000. "They've got children having sex together in this." The student was referring to *Brave New World*, which had been assigned to classes at Foley High School in Foley, Alabama, a small town near the Gulf Coast.

Stone filed a formal complaint with the school board, claiming that the novel depicted "orgies, self-flogging, suicide" and featured characters who displayed "contempt for religion, marriage, and the family." Stone didn't stop at the school board, however; she also brought up the matter with the governor of Alabama, Don Siegelman.

In September, school authorities removed the novel from the school's library, claiming it was not being banned, but only removed pending a full review.

Landmark Challenge:
Making Parents Matter in Mercedes

"This is pornographic literature, and we do not feel it has a place in any school funded by taxpayer dollars," wrote parent Julie Wilde, referring to *Brave New World* in a 2003 challenge in Mercedes, Texas. Huxley's novel was not the only book that Wilde and three other parents of sophomores at Science Academy wanted removed from the tenth-grade English Advanced Placement summer reading list. Robert Heinlein's science-fiction classic *Stranger in a Strange Land* was also challenged by the parents as possibly leading to "inappropriate sexual arousal of young teens," according to Wilde.

The high school's principal, following district policy, formed a committee to reassess the two books, which had been part of the curriculum for at least ten years. In June, the committee completed its reassessment and issued a report recommending both novels be retained in the curriculum. The committee claimed that the books had helped to develop students' Scholastic Aptitude Test (SAT) vocabulary and Advanced Placement analytical skills and played a role in making the Science Academy, according to a *Newsweek* magazine survey, the eighth-best high school in the country.

Nevertheless, the parents continued their challenge, taking it to the superintendent of schools in the South Texas Independent School District. He supported the committee's recommendation. Undeterred, the parents took their case to the district board of trustees. The board came to no decision at its August meeting and tabled the issue until September.

Before that meeting, the board received letters and messages from numerous supporters of the books. "The ethical and literary value of a work is distorted if one focuses only on particular words, passages, or segments," wrote Charles Suhor, field representative for the National Council of Teachers of English (NCTE), to the board. "An author's broad moral vision, total treatment of theme, and commitment to realistic portrayal of characters and dialogue are ignored when protesters focus only on aspects that are offensive to them. Unfortunately, there is shock value in isolating and listing selected passages from a book; but this does not reveal anything about the fundamental message or theme in the work, and it does not provide insight into its teachability or its literary quality."

At its meeting, the board voted to retain the books but required principals to offer alternatives to books from the reading list that parents could choose to have their child read instead.

Further Reading

American Library Association Web site. "Banned and/or Challenged Books from the Radcliffe Publishing Course Top 100 Novels of the 20th Century." Available online: www.ala.org/ala/oif/bannedbooks week/bbwlinks/reasonsbanned.htm. Accessed November 19, 2007.

Bedford, Sybille. *Aldous Huxley: A Biography*. New York: Knopf, 1974.

Foerstel, Herbert N. *Banned in the U.S.A.: A Reference Guide to Book Censorship in Schools and Public Libraries*. Westport, Conn.: Greenwood Press, 2002.

"Gallatin, Tennessee." *Newsletter on Intellectual Freedom*, March 1998: 49.

Sova, Dawn B. *Banned Books: Literature Suppressed on Social Grounds*. New York: Facts On File, 2006.

Zeleznik, Jennine. "Parents Seek to Ban Books." *McAllen Monitor Newspaper*, September 22, 2003. Available online: http://www.kythri.net/archives/000035.html. Accessed July 28, 2008.

About the Author of *Brave New World*

Aldous Huxley (1894–1963)

A leading British novelist and essayist of the twentieth century, Aldous Huxley was born on July 26, 1894, in Godalming, Surrey. His grandfather was the celebrated biologist and educator, Thomas Huxley, and his father, Leonard, was a biographer and magazine editor. Aldous's brother Julian also became a distinguished zoologist and writer, while his half-brother Andrew was a well-known physiologist and winner of the 1963 Nobel Prize in Physiology or Medicine.

Aldous himself studied medicine at Eton but gave it up when he was temporarily blinded by an eye disease at age sixteen.

He then turned to literature, publishing three collections of poetry and a volume of short stories before producing his first novel, *Crome Yellow*, in 1921. This book and other early novels were clever satires on British society of the 1920s. The best known of these books, *Point Counter Point* (1928), was a semi-autobiographical look at himself and his literary circle. In the 1930s, Huxley's fiction turned more fantastical, reflecting a growing interest in mysticism and science fiction. *Brave New World* (1932), considered his most savage satire, summed up his despair about the modern world.

Huxley moved to Southern California in 1937 with his Belgian-born wife and their son and became a permanent U.S. resident. He worked on a number of movie screenplays, receiving on-screen credit for the film *Pride and Prejudice* (1940), based on the classic Jane Austen novel. Huxley also wrote collections of essays, including *The Perennial Philosophy* (1945); *The Doors of Perception* (1954), which dealt with his experiments with mind-expanding drugs such as LSD; and *Literature and Science* (1963), his last published work.

Huxley died of cancer on November 22, 1963, in Los Angeles, California. His death was overshadowed by the assassination of President John F. Kennedy in Dallas, Texas, that same day.

Fahrenheit 451 (1953)
by Ray Bradbury

What Happens in *Fahrenheit 451*

Ray Bradbury's novel takes place in a futuristic world where the main goal of life is self-indulgent pleasure. In this paternalistic society, citizens are encouraged not to think for themselves, but rather to rely on the judgment of the controlling government. Ideas, and the books that espouse them, are outlawed. The job of finding and destroying books belongs to local fire departments. Firemen, in this topsy-turvy world, do not put out fires—they start them. Every fireman wears the number 451, the temperature in Fahrenheit at which paper burns, on his uniform.

Guy Montag is a loyal fireman who begins to have doubts about his position. Unlike his wife, Mildred, who spends much of her time watching television on three walls of their house, Guy feels that something is missing in his life. These feelings are confirmed when he meets Clarisse, a girl who loves to read. Guy's relationship with Clarisse leads him to begin reading books, and this opens up a new world for him.

Unfortunately, Montag's illegal activity is discovered by his superior, Captain Beatty, who forces Montag to burn his own home and the books in it. But Montag kills Beatty and then flees the city. An elaborate manhunt is conducted, but Montag eludes it and arrives at a place where a group of outsiders live. Each individual's goal here is to memorize a great novel to preserve literature for a future day when the present government falls. Montag decides to join them. As the book ends, a bomb destroys the city, and Montag and the other bookmen return to help rebuild the city.

Challenges and Censorship

It is irony of the highest kind that the most famous novel written about censorship should itself be a victim of the censorship it seeks to combat. Ray Bradbury began writing the novella, *The Fireman*, that would become *Fahrenheit 451*, in the spring of 1950, when he was twenty-nine years old. He completed a first draft in nine days, pecking away furiously at a rental typewriter in the basement of the University of California at Los Angeles (UCLA) library. *The Fireman* was published later that year in *Galaxy Science Fiction*, a pulp magazine. But Bradbury saw more in his futuristic fable and expanded the novella into the final novel, published in 1953.

The book struck a chord with readers and became Bradbury's most popular and famous work. By 2007, there were more than four million copies of *Fahrenheit 451* in print. A film adaptation by French director François Truffaut appeared in 1966, starring Oskar Werner as Guy Montag and Julie Christie in the double role of Mildred Montag and Clarisse. In 2007, *Match to Flame: The Fictional Paths to Fahrenheit 451*, was published, containing the original novella, drafts of the novel, and Bradbury's correspondence concerning the novel.

The numerous challenges to the book, which is frequently included in the high school English curriculum, are based on bad language, references to smoking cigarettes and drinking alcohol, and the author's pessimistic view of society and authority. Perhaps the most disturbing censorship of the novel took place in Venado Middle School in Irvine, California, in 1992. School officials there ordered teachers to black out with markers all "obscene words" (such as "hell" and "damn") in copies of the novel before distributing them to students for reading. When the story of the censorship got out in the press, it stirred so much controversy that the censored copies of the novel were quickly withdrawn.

Bradbury himself had the last word on censorship of his work in his "Coda to Fahrenheit 451," in which he wrote: "In sum, do not insult me with the beheadings, finger-choppings, or the lung-deflations you plan for my words. I need my head to shake or nod, my hands to wave or make into a fist, my lungs to shout or whisper with. I will not go gently onto a shelf, degutted, or become a non-book."

Landmark Challenge:
Betrayed by Ballantine Books

By 1979, Ray Bradbury was long familiar with school challenges and other forms of censorship against *Fahrenheit 451*. But nothing could have prepared him for the startling news from a friend that year that one of his own publishers had been censoring his book for thirteen years. In 1966, Ballantine Books came out with a special edition of Bradbury's novel for high school students. To avoid controversy in schools, the publisher took it upon itself to modify seventy-five passages, taking out bad language and controversial words such as "abortion." The author was not told of these changes and they were not documented on the copyright page. Ballantine continued to publish the unmodified adult version of the novel for six years. Then it dropped the adult version and published only the altered high school edition.

When he found out what the publisher had done, Bradbury was furious. He demanded that the high school edition be removed from sales and the original returned to print. Ballantine agreed to do so.

The incident had a positive effect. The American Library Association established a young-adult (YA) division of its Intellectual Freedom Committee, which began investigating the expurgation of literary classics by Scholastic Book Clubs and others. Its publicity of such tampering led to a publishing policy of clearly stating that an original work has been changed on the copyright page of such editions.

Landmark Challenge:
The Play's the Thing in Pylesville

What started as a stage adaptation of *Fahrenheit 451* at North Harford Middle School in Pylesville, Maryland, quickly turned into a larger-than-life drama that pitted the school's principal against the cast and sponsoring teachers.

Harry Hinman, the principal of North Harford, was not pleased with the language when he read the script of the play in April 1988. The production was allowed to go forward only after the publisher granted permission for the school to alter up to 100 lines containing what Hinman called "objectionable language." In the end, forty-one lines were changed for a performance for students, and thirty-nine lines were altered for an evening performance for parents and friends.

Thomas Berg and Virginia Huller, the two teachers sponsoring the production by the eighth-grade gifted and talented class, agreed to the forty-one changes for the in-school performance. But they requested that only thirty-three lines be changed for the evening performance, keeping several "hells" and "damns" in the dialogue. When Hinman refused their request, the teachers filed a grievance through the teachers' union.

"It is strange that the play about censorship would be one that we censored ourselves," said Huller. "We compromised our values to eliminate all but the references to 'hell' and 'damn.' It got down to the point that we either accepted it or the play would not be put on. The play is too important and the students have already worked too hard . . . The kids are living a real lesson by learning what censorship can really do."

This was not the first time that a play had brought controversy to the school. Four years earlier, a presentation of the play *Inherit the Wind*, about a 1920s trial regarding the teaching of evolution in schools, caused such an uproar that the school district formed a new policy calling for the review and approval of all school dramatic productions.

Landmark Challenge:
"All Kinds of Filth" in Conroe, Texas

Fifteen-year-old Diana Verm, a sophomore at Caney Creek High School, didn't like bad language any more than her father did. When she came to him in September 2006, concerned about her book assignment, *Fahrenheit 451*, he was ready to take up the matter with the school district.

"It's just all kinds of filth," Alton Verm wrote in his Request for Reconsideration of Instructional Materials. "The words don't need to be brought out in class. I want to get the book taken out of the class." Although he hadn't read the entire book, Verm found disturbing passages about drunkenness, cigarette smoking, "dirty talk," and anti-religious and anti-Biblical references.

His daughter and another classmate were allowed to read an alternative book, *Ella Minnow Pea*, by Mark Dunn, that deals with some of the same themes as *Fahrenheit 451*. When the rest of the class read or discussed Bradbury's book, the two students left the room.

Chris Hines, Conroe Independent School District's assistant superintendent for secondary education, defended *Fahrenheit 451*, which had been used in the district's curriculum for at least nineteen years. He called it an important book about society that students should be allowed to read. "They're not reading books just to read them," he said. "They're reading it for a purpose . . . We respect people's rights to express their concerns and we have a policy in place to handle that."

Ironically, Verm's challenge against *Fahrenheit 451*, the first challenge in the district in at least four years, occurred during the twenty-fifth annual Banned Books Week.

Further Reading

Beahm, George, ed. *War of Words: The Censorship Debate*. Kansas City, Mo.: Andrews & McMeel, 1993.

"Conroe, Texas." *Newsletter on Intellectual Freedom*, November 2006: 293. Available online: https://members.ala.org/nif/v55n6/dateline.html.

Jones, Derek, ed. *Censorship: A World Encyclopedia, Vol. 1 A–D*. London, England: Fitzroy Dearborn, 2001.

Micek, Kassia. "Parent Criticizes Book 'Fahrenheit 451.'" Houston Community Newspapers Online, October 1, 2006. Available online: www.hcnonline.com/articles/2006/10/01/import/20061001-archive119.txt. Accessed November 26, 2007.

"Pylesville, Maryland." *Newsletter on Intellectual Freedom*, July 1988: 123–124.

Ray Bradbury official website. Available online: www.raybradbury.com.

Shaftel, David. "Vintage Bradbury, Packaged Anew." *New York Times*, August 22, 2007: E1, E8. Available online: www.nytimes.com/2007/08/22/books/22brad.html.

About the Author of *Fahrenheit 451*

Ray Bradbury (1920–   )

Arguably the most popular and celebrated writer of adult fantasy in the twentieth century, Ray Bradbury was born on August 22, 1920, in Waukegan, Illinois. In 1939, at age eighteen, he self-published a fantasy magazine, *Futuria Fantasia*, that contained his own fiction and that of other fantasy writers. In his twenties, Bradbury began selling short stories to "pulp" magazines of science fiction and fantasy. He gained fame in 1950 with the publication of *The Martian Chronicles*, a collection of short stories built around the discovery of a lost civilization on the planet Mars. *The Illustrated Man* (1951) was another thematically related collection of stories. His first and most celebrated novel, *Fahrenheit 451*, appeared in 1953. Its story of the dehumanizing power of a technological society is a common theme in much of his work.

In the 1950s, Bradbury worked on a number of screenplays, the best-known being the screen version of Herman Melville's classic novel *Moby-Dick* (1956), directed by John Huston. His own space-age version of *Moby-Dick, Leviathan '99*, was published in a collection of never-released novellas in 2007. Other well-known works are the story collections *Dandelion Wine* (1957) and *A Medicine for Melancholy* (1959) and the novel *Something Wicked This Way Comes* (1962). Bradbury also wrote teleplays adapted from his stories for the television anthology series *Alfred Hitchcock Presents* (1955–67) and *The Twilight Zone* (1959–65), as well as his own program, *Ray Bradbury Theater* (1985–92).

Bradbury suffered a debilitating stroke in 1999 but continues to write, dictating over the telephone to his daughter in Arizona. He is the recipient of a World Fantasy Award for life achievement, and in 2007, he was awarded a special distinguished-career citation from the Pulitzer Prize Board.

As the prolific author said in one interview, "I'm accustomed, you see, to getting up every morning, running to the typewriter, and in an hour I've created a world."

Witches, Witches, Witches (1958) and Other Books about Witchcraft

by various authors and editors

What Happens in *Witches, Witches, Witches* and Other Books about Witchcraft

A Popular History of Witchcraft (1937) is a general survey of witchcraft written by Montague Summers, an English clergyman who focuses his study on English witches in the early twentieth century.

Witches, Witches, Witches (1958), edited by Helen Hoke, is a collection of poems and tales about witches written by such well-known authors as the Brothers Grimm, Oscar Wilde, and Oliver Wendell Holmes.

Buckland's Complete Book of Witchcraft (1986) is a classic introduction to Wicca, a nature-based, pre-Christian religion associated with witchcraft by one of its leading proponents in the United States, Raymond Buckland.

Halloween ABC (1987) is a collection of twenty-six poems by Eve Merriam about Halloween, witches, and other scary things, each highlighting one letter of the alphabet. The ghostly illustrations are by Lane Smith.

I Know I'm a Witch (1988), a children's picture book by David A. Adler and Suçie Stevenson, is about a little girl who, based on faulty evidence, mistakenly believes that she is a witch.

Witch Poems (1990), edited by Daisy Wallace, is an anthology of twenty poems about witches, magic spells, and the occult by writers such as poet e. e. cummings, *The Wizard of Oz* author, L. Frank Baum, and playwright William Shakespeare.

Challenges and Censorship

Books having to do with witches, witchcraft, and the occult have long been the most challenged kind of fantasy fiction and nonfiction in American schools and libraries. While only one of the books in this section has made any of the American Library Association's lists of most frequently challenged books, they have all been strenuously challenged in school districts around the country, both collectively and individually. The challenges have been made against true witchcraft books such as *A Popular History of Witchcraft* and *Buckland's Complete Book of Witchcraft*, as well as anthologies of poems and stories about witches (*Witches, Witches, Witches* and *Witch Poems*) and fictional books specifically written for children (*Halloween ABC* and *I Know I'm a Witch*). The challenges have focused on the threat to Christianity posed by witches and witchcraft, the promotion of witchcraft's dark practices to children, and the depiction of "violent criminal and deviant behavior" (in a challenge made against *Halloween ABC*). This last book ranked thirty-fourth on the ALA's "100 Most Frequently Challenged Books of 1990–2000."

Landmark Challenge:
The Minister's Wife

When Holly Hillman saw that a friend's eight-year-old daughter had checked out *Witches, Witches, Witches* from her school library in Smith Valley, Nevada, she decided to take action. Mary Ann Miller, the school librarian at the K–12 school, refused to remove the book, so Hillman took her complaint to a school review committee in March 1988. The fact that she was the wife of a Methodist minister gave her challenge added clout. "I've only been a Christian for ten years," she wrote, "but knowing my hippie view against violence, I would have felt the same way before. Our society is frightening enough with the threat of child abuse, AIDS, a nuclear holocaust, a fragile economy, environmental pollution, potential war in the Mideast. I do not see the need to add to a child's world view a fictitious book that is replete with scenes of intrusion, oppression, cannibalism, abduction, transformation, incantations, deceptions, threats, and sexism."

Miller staunchly defended her actions. "I believe in the First Amendment, not censorship," she said. "My decision was to retain the book on the shelf for other people to enjoy." Hillman countered that she wasn't seeking to have the book removed from the library but put in a special section "where a parent could say, 'I want my child to have that.'"

Among those following the story was Martha Gould, director of the Washoe County Library System in Reno, Nevada. "I can empathize with someone concerned about violence," she admitted. "Good heavens, they have a right and they should be commended when they care enough to say something. The question here, though, is one of perception. When you talk about removing books, it is a matter of personal perception, and the bottom line is that it is censorship, pure and simple."

On April 28, the review panel returned its verdict. According to panel member and Smith Valley School principal Russ Colletta, "The best interests of the students wouldn't be served by removing the book."

"I appreciate the time the librarians [on the committee] took, but no psychologists were included in the hearing," responded Hillman. "I would have wished that a psychologist could have made that decision."

Landmark Challenge: Three Students Take a Stand

Lloyd Kimsey, librarian at El Camino High School in Oceanside, California, must have been taken aback in late 1985, when three students came to him to request that he remove twenty-four books on the occult—which they felt glorified Satan—from the library's shelves. Kimsey refused their request, so they took it to a higher level.

Two of the students and one of their mothers, Shari Thomas, attended a meeting with district superintendent Steven Speech and principal Don Marks. "They filled out the proper form and listed the objectionable books and sections," reported Speech. The books in question included *A Popular History of Witchcraft*, by Montague Summers; *America Bewitched*; and the twenty-volume encyclopedia *Man, Myth & Magic*. Some of the books, such as *Witches*, were written to entertain and inform children and not to espouse witchcraft. But the student challengers were not convinced. "[A]lthough seemingly childish, [*Witches*] contains a lot of info on witch covens [an assembly of witches]," they wrote in their complaint. "This information can be easily used to form a coven."

"We're not rabble-rousers or censors," said Thomas, who owns a Christian bookstore. "I'm not after any books certified by the librarians' association or any literature ... But these books, with their graphic descriptions of how to practice witchcraft as a religion, is what disturbs us."

A committee was formed to consider the challenge.

Landmark Challenge:
No Picnic for Occult Books in Boulder

Pentecostal minister Phil Day announced the event to be held at his North Boulder, Colorado, church on February 20, 1988, as a picnic. However, the picnic was a ruse for a far more somber happening. "We'll have marshmallows and weenies," he told reporters beforehand, "but the books will provide the fuel." The books Day intended to burn all dealt with the occult, and he described them as "satanic."

Day's book burners were outnumbered about ten to one by some 200 protestors. Some of the demonstrators carried signs. One read: "Burning books is easy. Reading them takes intelligence." As the "picnic" got under way, the protesters overturned the barbecue grill and doused the flames with a water balloon. Day still managed to burn three of the dozens of books donated—*The Modern Witch's Handbook*, *Happy Birthday Planet Earth*, and actress Shirley MacLaine's autobiographical *Out on a Limb*, in which she professes belief in reincarnation.

Addressing the hostile crowd, Day declared, "We might be burning some books tonight, but soon God will be burning you." The confrontation between the book burners and book lovers never became physically violent, and the observing police made no arrests. Most of the remaining books were taken away by the protesters. The book burning led to a lengthy debate that went on for weeks and culminated in a public debate between Day; Ricki Seidman, legal defense of People for the American Way; and Gilbert Horn, executive director of the Colorado Council of Churches.

Landmark Challenge:
Not Just "A Little Halloween Book"

It wasn't on Halloween, but just before Christmas in 1992 when Kelly and Jeff Stone requested that *Witch Poems* be removed from the Irving School library in Bozeman, Montana, because it had frightened their kindergarten-age daughter. "I felt that it wasn't just a little Halloween book," complained Kelly Stone. "I found it was more of a satanic book. Can't our children be protected from demons and witches for a while longer? The book is neither entertaining nor educational and I wonder why it is in the library."

A committee composed of school librarians, a teacher, parents, and the district's community education director was ordered to consider the challenge and make a recommendation. When the committee held an open hearing in June 1993, a dozen people came forward to defend the anthology. "[I]t has only as much power as we give it," said the Rev. Denise Rogers, referring to the "satanic" content of the book. "It's only when we allow our children to question that we can strengthen them." "By any other name," declared parent George Robinson, "this is censorship."

The committee voted unanimously to retain *Witch Poems*.

Landmark Challenge:
A Hung Jury in Othello, Washington

School review committees usually come to some agreement for or against a book's removal, but such was not the case in Othello, Washington, in early 1993. The review committee, considering the challenge against Eve Merriam's *Halloween ABC*, was split three ways. Three members wanted to keep the book in schools with no restrictions. Two members wanted it restricted to older students. Two members, including challenger Noemi Ortega, wanted it out of all school libraries.

Seeing that no clear decision could be reached, superintendent of schools Dennis Carter ruled on the basis of previous court decisions to keep *Halloween ABC* in schools. Ortega and other parents gathered more than 600 signatures on a petition opposing the book and took it to the Othello school board. Ortega called the scary poems "violent" and claimed the book promoted criminal behavior.

For more than an hour, the school board listened to testimony from challengers and supporters of the book. When the talk ended, the board members voted and, unlike the review committee, they were in agreement. They voted 5 to 0 to keep *Halloween ABC*. People came to the United States because "we cherish the right to choose and the opportunities of freedom this great country has given us," said board chairman Duane Van Beek.

"Who are you people?" asked a disappointed Ortega. "We are parents. We are here to help our school district."

Landmark Challenge: A Library's Unwanted Donations

When the Seabrook Public Library in Seabrook, New Hampshire, announced two summer lectures for young adults in 1996, it had no idea what a firestorm of controversy it would lead to.

The announcement of the lectures—"The History and Use of Tarot Cards" and "Numerology and Dream Analysis"—brought forth an angry letter from the Rev. Andrew Gosnell of the Rand Memorial Congregational Church to the library's trustees, demanding that they cancel the two lectures or risk "inviting all who would participate to unleash a literal 'hornet's nest' of destructive spiritual entities into their lives."

The board offered to reschedule the lectures for adults only, but this did not appease Gosnell and his 300 churchgoing supporters. "There is a power at work in these tarot readings and the like, but it's not the power of God," said Gosnell's colleague, the Rev. Elizabeth Walton. "If people want to learn about tarot cards, let them go to one of those stores in Portsmouth or hire a hall someplace for their lecture."

But 250 town residents supported the lectures and signed an anti-censorship petition. "The library is a place for controversy," said Teresa Amato, who helped circulate the petition. "Democracy depends on it, and on the free flow of information, not denying people the right to make their own choices."

The library board finally voted 2 to 1 to postpone nearly all library programs, pending the formation of a policy for lecture topics. Head librarian Elizabeth Heath felt betrayed by the board and believed that the lectures should have been held as scheduled. What happened next left her and her staff completely "dazed and confused."

Tom Canfield, who worked for a New Age publishing house in York, Maine, shared Heath's concern for free speech. "I felt a sense of outrage that these lectures were banned," he said. "It's censorship, pure and simple." In response, Canfield posted the news of the forced postponement on the Internet and urged people to show their displeasure by donating books on the occult to the library. Soon, the Seabrook Library was being inundated daily with books sent through the mail, including a copy of *Buckland's Complete Book of Witchcraft*. Before it was over, the library had received nearly 500 books, all of them related to the occult, enough to fill a seven-foot-high bookcase.

And what was the library going to do with these unrequested donations? "Some of the titles I saw looked excellent," reported Heath. "We'll definitely keep some of them."

Landmark Challenge:
"A Potentially Dangerous Thing"

The little girl in David A. Adler's book *I Know I'm a Witch* isn't really a witch at all, but Jennifer Craven of Hanover Park, Illinois, took her desire to be one very seriously. She didn't want her daughter, in kindergarten at Prairie View Elementary School in Elgin, or any other student reading it. "I feel that at my daughter's age I can step in," she told district officials in December 1997. "Next year, when she's a proficient reader and pulls a book off the shelf, I won't always be able to step in. The argument is that witchcraft is a very potentially dangerous thing. Why, if it's potentially dangerous, would we have it?"

But an Elgin Area Unit District 46 commission that examined the challenge disagreed. On January 29, 1998, it voted unanimously to keep *I Know I'm a Witch* on school library shelves. "I believe censorship is the most dangerous thing in the world when we practice this outside the home," said Sue Bernardi, commission chair. "I think this book is totally tongue-in-cheek and very playful. That's the beauty of literature. I interpret it one way, you interpret it another way."

Because everyone can view a book differently, the commission reasoned, no one should have the right to tell other people they can't read it. "We have thousands of books that families want and read, but some parents find them offensive," said middle school librarian Jan Barry. "However, we must represent the needs of the community and not say one parent has the right over another."

Further Reading

"Boulder, Colorado." *Newsletter on Intellectual Freedom*, May 1988: 92–93.

"Bozeman, Montana." *Newsletter on Intellectual Freedom*, September 1993: 158.

"Dispute on Tarot Lecture Roils a Small-Town Library." *New York Times*, November 30, 1996: 1:13. Available online: http://query.nytimes.com/gst/fullpage.html?res=9B03E6D7153CF933A05752C1A960958260&sec=&spon=&partner=permalink&exprod=permalink.

"Elgin, Illinois." *Newsletter on Intellectual Freedom*, May 1998: 87.

"Oceanside, California." Newsletter on Intellectual Freedom, September 1986: 151.

"Othello, Washington." *Newsletter on Intellectual Freedom*, September 1993: 159.

Pistolis, Donna Reidy, ed. *Hit List: Frequently Challenged Books for Children*. Chicago: American Library Association, 1996.

"Seabrook, New Hampshire." *Newsletter on Intellectual Freedom*, March 1997: 36–37.

"Smith Valley, Nevada." *Newsletter on Intellectual Freedom*, July 1988: 121–122; September 1988: 178.

About the Authors and Editors of Witch Books

Montague Summers (1880–1948), *A Popular History of Witchcraft*
An eccentric English clergyman and author, Summers wrote a number of books about witches, vampires, and werewolves, as well as a famous translation of the medieval witch hunter's manual *The Malleus Maleficarum*. He also published prose, poetry, and plays.

Helen Hoke (1903–1990), *Witches, Witches, Witches*
A writer and editor, Hoke also edited the books *Terrors, Torments, and Traumas* (1978) and *Mysterious, Menacing, and Macabre* (1981).

**Raymond Buckland (1934–   ),
*Buckland's Complete Book of Witchcraft***
Born in London on August 31, 1934, Buckland immigrated to the United States in 1962. He claims to be the first person in the United States to admit to practicing Wicca, the pagan religion associated with witches. He lives in Wooster, Ohio, and has written numerous books on the occult.

Eve Merriam (1916–1992), *Halloween ABC*

One of the most celebrated children's poets of twentieth-century America, Eve Merriam was born on July 19, 1916, in Philadelphia, Pennsylvania. She attended Cornell University and the University of Pennsylvania. Her first book of poems, *Family Circle*, was published in 1946. Among her best-known books of poetry are *It Doesn't Always Have to Rhyme* (1964), *The Inner City Mother Goose* (1969), and *Out Loud* (1973). Merriam was the recipient of the 1981 National Council of Teachers of English (NCTE) Award for Excellence in Poetry for Children. She died of cancer on April 11, 1992.

David A. Adler (1947–   ), *I Know I'm a Witch*

Adler was born on April 10, 1947, in New York City. A former math teacher, he is the author of approximately 200 books for children and young adults. He is best known for the *Cam Jansen* mystery series, but he has also written biographies and books on science and math. "Because of the diversity of the books I write, I am able to vary my work even in a single day from research on a nonfiction book to fiction writing to riddle writing," Adler has said.

Daisy Wallace (1948–   ), *Witch Poems*

Daisy Wallace is the pseudonym of Margery Cuyler. She was born in Princeton, New Jersey, and earned a B.A. degree from Sarah Lawrence College in 1970. In addition to editing several other poetry anthologies for children under the name Daisy Wallace, Cuyler has published numerous picture books and several books for older children under her real name.

James and the Giant Peach (1961)
by Roald Dahl

What Happens in *James and the Giant Peach*

Four-year-old James Henry Trotter is left an orphan when his parents are eaten by a rhinoceros that escaped from the London Zoo. James goes to live with his two cruel aunts, Spiker and Sponge. They treat him miserably, and he longs to escape from them. At age seven, James meets a mysterious old man who gives him a sack containing magic green crystals that the man says will bring him happiness. While running home with the sack, James stumbles and the crystals spill onto the ground near a barren peach tree, immediately disappearing. James thinks all is lost, but soon afterward, the peach tree sprouts a peach that grows and grows to gigantic size.

Spiker and Sponge take advantage of the situation and sell tickets to people to view the giant peach. One night, James crawls inside the peach and encounters a strange group of giant-sized insects who befriend him. They include a silkworm, glowworm, centipede, and two females—Miss Spider and Mrs. Ladybug. With some help from the centipede, the peach breaks off the tree and rolls down an embankment, flattening and killing the two aunts.

Then the peach rolls into the Atlantic Ocean. James and his new-found friends plan to sail in their sea-borne peach to New York City to start new lives. Along the way they have numerous adventures, including a run-in with a group of hungry sharks. James saves them from the sharks by tying silk strands from the silkworm and Miss Spider's webbing to 502 seagulls. The gulls lift the peach out of the water and high into the sky.

Later the occupants of the giant peach are almost destroyed by huge Cloud Men, but they escape their clutches and finally land at their destination—New York City. The peach is speared by the needle atop the Empire State Building. The mayor of New York City throws a ticker-tape parade for James and his insect friends. As the parade progresses down Fifth Avenue, hungry children devour the giant peach. The peach stone is installed in New York's Central Park and becomes James's new home, where he is visited by many new friends and admirers. They all want to hear about his amazing adventures, which he decides to write down—in the very book being read.

Challenges and Censorship

Since its publication in 1961, *James and the Giant Peach* has been hailed as a modern classic of children's literature. But like many of Roald Dahl's books for young readers, it has also earned its share of criticism and challenges. The violent death of James's two nasty aunts and the references to chewing tobacco and whiskey drinking have been the reasons for many of the challenges.

James and the Giant Peach ranked fifty-sixth on the American Library Association's "100 Most Frequently Challenged Books of 1990–2000." Dahl ranked seventh on People for the American Way's "Most Frequently Challenged Authors 1982–1996."

Dahl himself was quick to point out that children who wrote to him about *James* and his other books always liked the "gruesome events" the best. "They don't relate it to life," he insisted. "They enjoy the fantasy. And my nastiness is never gratuitous. It's retribution. Beastly people must be punished."

Landmark Challenge:
Crocodile Tongues and Lizard Eyeballs

"The whole book is strange if you ask me," stated Teresa Calitri, whose daughter was given *James and the Giant Peach* to read in a fourth-grade class at Deep Creek Elementary School in Charlotte Harbor, Florida. In her April 1991 letter to the editor of the *Charlotte Sun Herald*, she wrote, "I know there are people who agree that this is not an appropriate reading lesson for children. So have an influence in the shaping of their lives by calling the school and telling them."

Oddly, that is exactly what Calitri herself failed to do. Neither Deep Creek principal Peggy M. Jividen nor Calitri's daughter's teacher heard from her about the book. Her daughter, however, did write to her teacher, explaining that she could not read the book. The teacher gave her an alternate reading assignment.

Calitri's complaint focused on a witch's spell in the book that included "one thousand long slimy crocodile tongues boiled up in the skull of a dead witch for twenty days and nights with the eyeballs of a lizard!" In her response she wrote, rather strangely, "If they're going to teach witchcraft, I think they should teach the whole thing. Witchcraft is no joke."

Principal Jividen and county director of special projects Janet A. Williams saw *James and the Giant Peach* not as a book about witchcraft but rather as an imaginative children's classic that should remain in the school. "Literature exposes students to a variety of ideas," Williams said. "That's what democracy is all about. The purpose of education is not only to communicate factual information, but to develop in the young the ability to discriminate and choose."

Landmark Challenge: Reacting to an "Ass" in Altoona

"Of course I'm not talking to you, you ass!" the ill-tempered centipede yelled at James. That was enough for Teresa Root to request that the book be removed from the reading list at Pedersen Elementary School in Altoona, Wisconsin.

"I couldn't believe my son was reading this to me," she wrote to the school board. "He looked at me and told me that if he used words like this around the house, I'd send him to his room. I'm not asking that book be taken off the library shelves. Parents can monitor what their children take out of the library. I just want children and their parents to have a choice of what kind of books they read."

It wasn't just the use of the word "ass" that disturbed Root when her nine-year-old son brought the book home. At another point in the story, the centipede sings a song about monkeys that chewed tobacco and hens that took snuff and porcupines that drank "fiery wines." Root also mentioned a word used to describe Mrs. Spider that she claimed "can be taken two ways, but I feel it's implied to be sexual."

A nine-member reconsideration committee reviewed Root's request and voted unanimously to keep the book in the school library. On December 3, 1991, the Altoona school board also voted unanimously to uphold the committee's decision. While agreeing that any parent has the right to review material and request that their children read alternative material, superintendent of schools Jon Lamberson drew the line at censorship. "According to board policy no parent has the right to exclude material from other students in the district and I think that's a very fair standard," he said.

Further Reading

"Altoona, Wisconsin." *Newsletter on Intellectual Freedom*, March 1992: 65.

Becker, Beverly C., and Susan M. Stan. *Hit List for Children 2: Frequently Challenged Books*. Chicago: American Library Association, 2002.

"Charlotte Harbor, Florida." *Newsletter on Intellectual Freedom*, July 1991: 108.

Green, Jonathon, and Nicholas J. Karolides. *Encyclopedia of Censorship, New Edition*. New York: Facts On File, 2005.

Sova, Dawn. *Banned Books: Literature Suppressed on Social Grounds*. New York: Facts On File, 2006.

About the Author of *James and the Giant Peach*

Roald Dahl (1916–1990)

Roald Dahl's strange and eccentric imagination has produced memorable stories of the macabre for both adults and children. Dahl was born in Llandaff, Wales (part of Great Britain), on September 13, 1916. His father and sister died when he was three. His mother sent him to a succession of boarding schools in England, where he was often lonely and unhappy. He spent his summers visiting relatives in his mother's homeland of Norway.

In 1934, Dahl went to work as a distributor for Shell Petroleum Company and was sent to Tanganyika (now Tanzania), in Africa. At the start of World War II, Dahl joined the Royal Air Force (RAF) and became a pilot officer. He survived a plane crash and shot down at least five enemy planes. When the war ended, he was a Wing Commander.

Dahl's first published work was the article "Shot Down over Libya," about his wartime experiences. The *Saturday Evening Post* bought it for $900. It was the start of a successful writing career. *Over to You: Ten Stories of Flyers and Flying* was published in 1946. His reputation as a short story writer of macabre tales with O. Henry—like twist endings was solidified with two collections, *Someone Like You* (1952) and *Kiss Kiss* (1960).

After the success of *James and the Giant Peach* (1961), Dahl concentrated most of his energies on children's books that were just as fantastical and often as gruesome as his adult fiction. Among his best-known children's books are *Charlie and the Chocolate Factory* (1964), *Fantastic Mr. Fox* (1970), *The BFG (Big Friendly Giant)* (1982), *The Witches* (1983), and *Matilda* (1988). He published another volume of adult stories, *Switch Bitch*, in 1974, and *Roald Dahl: Collected Stories* came out posthumously in 2006. Many of Dahl's stories have been adapted for television and appeared on *Alfred Hitchcock Presents* (1955–65), *Way Out* (1961), and *Tales of the Unexpected* (1979–81). Dahl was the droll host of the latter two programs.

He married film actress Patricia Neal in 1953 and had five children with her. The couple divorced in 1983 after Neal discovered her husband's long-term affair with her best friend, Felicity d'Abreu Crosland. He married Crosland soon after the divorce. Roald Dahl died of a rare blood disease at the age of seventy-four on November 23, 1990.

A Wrinkle in Time (1962)
by Madeleine L'Engle

What Happens in *A Wrinkle in Time*

Meg Murry, a sensitive young girl, is haunted by the disappearance of her scientist father. Years before, Dr. Murry left on a secret mission into the fifth dimension and was never seen again. An outcast from society because of her missing father and her intellectual abilities, Meg decides to go in search of him with her younger brother, Charles Wallace, and her friend Calvin O'Keefe.

Three celestial creatures—Mrs. Whatsit, Mrs. Who, and Mrs. Which—tell the three children about a tesseract, a "wrinkle" in space and time that will allow them to travel into the fifth dimension in search of Meg's father. They then help to transport the children to Camazotz, one of several planets that has been taken over by the Dark Thing, a powerful force of evil. It is here where Dr. Murry is being held captive.

Camazotz is controlled by IT, a huge brain without a body, which overpowers Charles and transforms him into a human robot that leads Meg and Calvin to Dr. Murry. Meg's father is able to escape with Meg and Calvin through a wrinkle in time. They arrive on Ixchel, a planet where tall, friendly, fur-covered creatures care for the time travelers. Charles remains a prisoner on Camazotz.

The three Mrs. Ws reappear on Ixchel and convince Meg that she must return alone to Camazotz to rescue Charles. They insist that she has a weapon more powerful than IT's evil, but she must discover it for herself. Only when Meg confronts the giant brain does she realize that the weapon she has is her capacity to love. She rescues Charles by concentrating on her love for him and thus vanquishes IT. The two children are "tessered" through time and space and home to Earth. Here they are reunited with Dr. Murry and Calvin, who had returned to Earth earlier.

Challenges and Censorship

A Wrinkle in Time has been called by one parent challenger "a thinly veiled pseudo-science fiction effort to inculcate my child in the occult." The many challenges against the novel have been based in large part on its humanistic, so-called "anti-Christian" message. Ironically, its author, Madeleine L'Engle, was a devout Christian who for thirty years served as librarian at the Episcopal landmark church in Manhattan, the Cathedral of St. John the Divine. A number of her later works, such as *A Stone for a Pillow: Journeys with Jacob* (1986), were based on biblical characters and themes.

L'Engle was inspired to write *A Wrinkle in Time* during a ten-week family camping trip. "I cannot possibly tell you how I came to write it," she once said. "It was simply a book I had to write. I had no choice. It was only after it was written that I realized what some of it meant."

The manuscript was rejected by twenty-six publishers before Farrar, Straus & Giroux agreed to publish it. Once in print, critics praised *A Wrinkle in Time* as an outstanding novel. It won the Newbery Medal in 1963 and was runner-up for the prestigious Hans Christian Andersen Award in 1964. It reached its sixty-ninth printing in 2007, at which point the book had sold eight million copies.

But the fantasy and the moral lessons it dramatizes have been attacked by many people, especially fundamentalist Christians who regard its humanistic approach to religiosity as heretical. It has also been accused of promoting witchcraft and the occult. *A Wrinkle in Time* ranked twenty-second on the American Library Association's "100 Most Frequently Challenged Books of 1990–2000."

L'Engle had mixed feelings about the frequent challenges against her novel. "I was really 'in' because people were condemning [it]," she said. "But they were Christians, mostly, and that made me very sad." Explaining the religious differences between her and her critics, she said that "the Fundalets [as she called the fundamentalists] want a closed system, and I want an open system." On the matter of book banning, she said, "You have got to be very careful of banning.

What you ban is not going to hurt anybody, usually. But the act of banning is."

One California parent paid L'Engle's powers of imagination a backhanded compliment when the person declared that her most famous novel is "frightening, [it] makes you believe in make believe."

Landmark Challenge: Taking the Lord's Name in Vain in Alabama

Putting Jesus Christ in her novel wasn't what got author Madeleine L'Engle in trouble in Anniston, Alabama. It was the company she put him in. In one passage in *A Wrinkle in Time*, L'Engle put Jesus on a list of defenders of Earth against evil that included great artists, scientists, philosophers, and religious leaders. For parent Tom Price, placing the son of God's name alongside mere mortals was akin to blasphemy. For this and other reasons, Price asked the school board on November 15, 1990, to remove it from elementary schools and not allow students to purchase copies in the classroom.

School superintendent Bruce Wright defended the book and pointed out that Price's nine-year-old son was among the many students in his class and others who wanted the book and purchased it before it was taught in class. At a December meeting, the Anniston Board of Education voted to support Wright's stand and not ban the book. But by then Price had already withdrawn his son from public school and had enrolled him in a Christian school, where he would be safe from any further exposure to books of fantasy.

Landmark Challenge: Something "More Dangerous" than Censorship

Ed Palmer's fifth-grade daughter was academically gifted, but that didn't mean he wanted her exposed to books that dealt with the occult and mysticism, words he used to describe *A Wrinkle in Time*. The girl told her father that she didn't like the novel and, after taking a look at the book for himself, he quickly agreed with her. Palmer's daughter had already been allowed to choose another book for the assignment, but he felt that other students should not be subjected to *A Wrinkle in Time* either.

In late 1995, Palmer wrote a letter of complaint to the Catawba County school board in Newton, North Carolina. Other parents vehemently opposed him. "Allowing this kind of censorship to take place is far more dangerous that anything you'd find in this book," said parent Susan Rittiner. Two school district committees independently reviewed the book and found it acceptable. Their recommendation went to the school board.

On January 29, 1996, the board voted unanimously to reject Palmer's request. Even Tim Goff, a self-described conservative member of the school board, said that while he could understand Palmer's concerns, "I believe the appropriate way to handle them is for him not to let his son or daughter read the book."

Further Reading

"Anniston, Alabama." *Newsletter on Intellectual Freedom*, March 1991: 62.

Becker, Beverly C., and Susan M. Stan. *Hit List for Children 2: Frequently Challenged Books*. Chicago: American Library Association, 2002.

Foerstel, Herbert N. *Banned in the U.S.A.: A Reference Guide to Book Censorship in Schools and Public Libraries*. Westport, Conn.: Greenwood Press, 2002.

Green, Jonathon, and Nicholas J. Karolides. *Encyclopedia of Censorship, New Edition*. New York: Facts On File, 2005.

Martin, Douglas. "Madeleine L'Engle, Author of the Classic 'A Wrinkle in Time,' Is Dead at 88." *New York Times*, September 8, 2007: A13. Available online: www.nytimes.com/2007/09/08/books/07cnd-lengle.html. Accessed January 3, 2008.

"Newton, North Carolina." *Newsletter on Intellectual Freedom*, May 1996: 97–98.

Zammarelli, Chris. "Faith Is Best Expressed in Story." Bookslut.com, June 2004. Available online: www.bookslut.com/banned_bookslut/2004_06_002633.php. Accessed January 3, 2008.

About the Author of *A Wrinkle in Time*

Madeleine L'Engle (1918–2007)

A pioneer in the field of children's literature, Madeleine L'Engle wrote novels filled with the wonder of the imagination that had real messages for young readers. She was born on November 29, 1918, in New York City and was raised an only child. Her father fought in World War I and was a journalist and arts critic for the *New York Sun*. Madeleine wrote her first story at age five, and she won a poetry contest in the fifth grade. She studied English at Smith College in Massachusetts and graduated with honors.

Upon returning to New York City, L'Engle wrote plays and acted on the stage. Her first novel, *The Small Rain*, was published in 1945. The following year, she married actor Hugh Franklin. In 1951, the couple moved to Goshen, Connecticut, with their daughter, Josephine, and operated a general store. They had a son in 1952 and adopted a second daughter four years later.

Frustrated by her lack of success in writing, L'Engle nearly quit the profession at age forty. But she persevered and found fame and celebrity with the publication of *A Wrinkle in Time* in 1962. She wrote numerous other books, including the five-book series about the Austin family. One of her last books was the autobiographical *Madeleine L'Engle Herself: Reflections on a Writing Life* (2001). From 1966 to 1996 she served as writer-in-residence and librarian at the Cathedral of St. John the Divine in New York City. She died at the age of eighty-eight on September 6, 2007, in a nursing home in Litchfield, Connecticut.

"Why does anybody tell a story?" L'Engle once asked. "It does indeed have something to do with faith, faith that the universe has meaning, that our little human lives are not irrelevant, that what we choose or say or do matters, matters cosmically."

In the Night Kitchen (1970)
by Maurice Sendak

What Happens in *In the Night Kitchen*

Mickey, a young boy, is awakened in what appears to be a dream and enters the fantastical Night Kitchen. Naked, Mickey falls into a bowl of unfinished cake batter presided over by three jolly bakers, each of whom resembles the movie comedian Oliver Hardy of the famous team of Laurel and Hardy. Mickey emerges from the batter, encrusted in bread dough. He fashions an airplane out of the baking dough and flies it into the night sky. Mickey falls from the plane into a giant milk bottle, and he then pours the milk into the cake batter, allowing the grateful bakers to finish the morning cake and deposit it into the oven. At daybreak, Mickey is back in his bed "cakefree and dried." He awakes with the happy knowledge that he will be able to have "cake every morning" for breakfast, thanks to his own ingenuity.

Challenges and Censorship

First published in 1970, *In the Night Kitchen* has been both praised and criticized from the beginning. One writer called it "[t]he perfect combination of a text based in the literary tradition of nursery rhymes and illustrations executed in a 1930-ish, art-deco style [that] evokes the comforting smells and decor of a homey, family kitchen."

But for some critics and readers, the best word to describe the picture book is not "homey," but "controversial." The most controversial feature, and one that has brought the majority of challenges against the book in schools and libraries, is the depicted nudity of the central character, a mischievous boy named Mickey. At least four times in the course of the story, Mickey is shown in full frontal nudity. According to writer Matthew Z. Heintzelman, it was the first time that an anatomically correct naked boy was depicted in a children's picture book.

The nudity has led to other disturbing challenges. In one picture, Mickey is shown pulling on the propeller of his bread dough airplane, which some challengers have seen as a reference to masturbation. On another spread, the three adult bakers are watching the naked Mickey pouring milk, which critics have read as a suggestion of child pornography. One challenge in Elk River, Minnesota, in 1992 declared that the book could "lay the foundation for future use of pornography."

All this may well have stunned the author, who sees the story as an autobiographical study of his own childhood and the successful empowerment of a child facing the adult world.

In the Night Kitchen ranked twenty-fifth on the American Library Association's "100 Most Frequently Challenged Books of 1990–2000." It also ranked seventh on the ALA's "10 Most Frequently Challenged Books of 2004" for reasons of "nudity and offensive language."

Landmark Challenges: Clothing Mickey

Mickey's nudity in *In the Night Kitchen* so bothered some librarians and teachers in what they considered an otherwise quite acceptable book that they decided to do something about it. Rather than ban the book, they merely cleaned it up by removing what offended them: they drew clothes on Mickey. One of the earliest examples of this willful defacement of the book occurred in Caldwell Parish Library, Louisiana, in 1972. The librarian, fearing that library patrons would object to the boy's nudity, simply painted a diaper with white tempera paint onto each illustration where Mickey appeared nude.

Five years later, two school officials took similar action in Springfield, Missouri. Again, it was "community standards" that director of curriculum development Howard Lowe hoped to protect by clothing little Mickey. "Obviously we felt there would be a reaction [to

Mickey's nudity]," said Lowe, "so we decided that if the book could be changed without altering it severely, we would do it." His partner in the cause was director of elementary education Wanda Gray, a self-professed "old fogey" on the issue of nudity. She, too, wanted only to respect the "feelings of people."

In 1994, a mother in El Paso, Texas, challenged the book in the local public library, declaring to the librarian that "[m]y son and I were offended by the fact the little boy pictured did not have any clothes on and it pictured his private area." The book, she claimed, "discourages family reading time." The library rejected her complaint, and the book stayed on its shelves.

Such challenges and expurgations led the ALA's Intellectual Freedom Committee to draft a statement entitled "Expurgation of Library Materials: An Interpretation of the Library Bill of Rights." The statement declared that "any deletion, excision, alteration, editing, or obliteration of any part(s) of books or other library resources by the library, its agent, or its parent institute (if any)" is a violation of the document.

Sendak has also spoken out strongly against the expurgators. "They are trying to keep their children in the dark about their own bodies," he once wrote. ". . . It's as if my book contains secret information that kids would be better off not knowing. This whole idea, of course, is ridiculous. Kids take an interest in their genitals at a very early age and are generally quite open about expressing this interest. It's only after they are made to feel ashamed of their bodies that they stop being so open."

Further Reading

Becker, Beverly C., and Susan M. Stan. *Hit List for Children 2: Frequently Challenged Books*. Chicago: American Library Association, 2002.

"Elk River, Minnesota." *Newsletter on Intellectual Freedom*, March 1993: 41.

"El Paso, Texas." *Newsletter on Intellectual Freedom*, September 1994: 148.

Heintzelman, Matthew Z. "Thirty Years without Diapers: Expurgating and Censoring Maurice Sendak's *In the Night Kitchen*." Available online: http://mingo.info-science.uiowa.edu/~heintzelman/thirty years.htm#_Toc507603127. Accessed December 14, 2007.

About the Author of *In the Night Kitchen*

Maurice Sendak (1928–   )

Maurice Sendak is one of the most respected and honored of children's authors and illustrators today. He was born on June 10, 1928, in Brooklyn, New York, to Polish-Jewish immigrants. After seeing the Disney animated movie *Fantasia* when he was twelve years old, Sendak was inspired to become an illustrator. His first published illustrations appeared in the 1947 textbook *Atomics for the Millions*. Through the 1950s, he drew illustrations for comic books and then began to illustrate children's books written by others.

Sendak's first great success as an author-illustrator was *Where the Wild Things Are* (1963), which won a Caldecott Medal in 1964. Sendak continued his exploration of children's fantastic and emotional needs in *In the Night Kitchen* (1970). His trilogy of books on this issue was completed with the less successful *Outside Over There* (1981).

Besides books, Sendak has contributed to other media, particularly film, television, and theater. As a member of the National Board of Advisors for the Children's Television Workshop, he helped develop the popular children's television show Sesame Street and created the musical *Really Rosie* with songwriter/singer Carole King, which was made into an animated television special in 1975.

He has also designed sets for numerous operas and ballets, including award-winning sets for the Pacific Northwest Ballet's production of Tchaikovsky's *The Nutcracker*. In 2003, Sendak illustrated playwright Tony Kushner's adaptation of a Czech children's opera, *Brundibar*, which was later produced on stage. In 2006, Sendak produced his first pop-up book, *Mommy?*

Sendak was the recipient of the Hans Christian Andersen Award for children's book illustration in 1970 and shared the first Astrid Lindgren Memorial Award with Austrian children's author Christine Nöstlinger in 2003.

The Stupids Books (1974–1989)
by Harry Allard

What Happens in *The Stupids* Books

The Stupids are an incredibly dense family of foolish people made up of Stanley Q. Stupid, his wife, son Buster, and daughter Petunia. They also have a dog named Kitty and a cat named Xylophone. Their humorous adventures are retold in four books.

In *The Stupids Step Out* (1974), the family takes a bath without water so their clothes won't get wet. Later they go out for mashed-potato sundaes with butterscotch syrup. When they come home and go to bed, their toes stick out from the covers where their heads should be.

In *The Stupids Have a Ball* (1978), Mr. and Mrs. Stupid decide to celebrate the fact that Buster and Petunia have flunked all their subjects at school by throwing a costume ball. Mr. Stupid dresses up as General George Washing Machine, and their dog masquerades as the Bone Ranger. Grandfather Stupid comes down the chimney dressed as the Easter Bunny.

In *The Stupids Die* (1981), a fuse blows and the lights go out while the family is watching television. They think they have died and gone to heaven.

In their last adventure, *The Stupids Take Off* (1989), they go on vacation to escape an annoying relative and visit such other colorful family members as Uncle Artichoke and Farmer Joe, who raises pencils.

Challenges and Censorship

"Good-natured *dummkopfs*" is what the *School Library Journal* reviewer called the Stupids upon publication of the first book of their adventures, in 1974. Since then, they have become one of the most popular of children's picture-book series, delighting several generations of young readers with their nonsensical antics. Writer Leonard Marcus called them "a family of noodleheads whose talent for getting backward what every four-year-old can plainly understand is matched only by their boundless *joie de vivre* [love of life]."

But their silliness has not pleased parents and other adults who have challenged the books, mostly in school and public libraries. They have complained about the family's odd behavior, their serving as poor role models for children, and their undermining of authority. As one 1985 challenge put it, the books "describe families in a derogatory manner and might encourage children to disobey their parents."

The *Stupids* books cumulatively ranked twenty-sixth on the American Library Association's "100 Most Frequently Challenged Books of 1990–2000." A very loose film adaptation of the books, directed by John Landis and starring Tom Arnold as Mr. Stupid, appeared in 1996 to dismal reviews and poor box-office sales.

Landmark Challenge: Name Calling in Zeeland

It wasn't just the content of the *The Stupids Die* that bothered parent Connie Beukema, but the family's name, which for her was a bad example for children who might call others stupid. Beukema made her request to have the book removed from the Howard Miller Library in Zeeland, Michigan, after hearing her nine-year-old daughter read it to her siblings. "I would rather have kids help each other and build them up," she told the library's advisory board.

In a meeting in June 1998, the board voted 4 to 0 to keep the book and the others in the series in circulation. "So far I don't see enough reasons to pull the book," claimed board president Allen Dannenberg. "In my opinion right now it stays on the shelf."

"My feeling is the library is not in a position to be the parental controller," said Bill Verplank, another board member. "I would want parents to be aware what their children have access to in the library."

Library director Tara Conaway felt Beukema's reasoning for her challenge was faulty. "Their name is Stupid," she explained. "The characters are not being called names."

Beukema accepted the board's decision, but did not regret making her challenge. "I didn't feel right not doing anything about it," she said. "Maybe this is a small thing we can do. Maybe you can not repurchase the books."

This was not the first time The *Stupids* books were challenged in Zeeland. Four years earlier, a group of parents had requested the books be banned from public school libraries. The Zeeland Board of Education rejected their request.

Further Reading

Becker, Beverly C., and Susan M. Stan. *Hit List for Children 2: Frequently Challenged Books*. Chicago: American Library Association, 2002.

Lambert, Bruce. "James Marshall, 50, an Illustrator and an Author for Children, Dies." *New York Times*, October 15, 1992: B16. Available online: http://query.nytimes.com/gst/fullpage.html?res=9E0CE7D71 33BF936A25753C1A964958260&sec=&spon=&partner=permalink &exprod=permalink. Accessed January 5, 2008.

Van Kolken, Paul. "The Stupids Stay On." *Holland Sentinel*, June 9, 1998.

About the Author of the *Stupids* Books

Harry Allard (1928–   )

A prolific author of humorous children's books, Harry Allard was born on January 27, 1928, in Evanston, Illinois. He majored in art at Northwestern College, graduating in 1943. After joining the Army, he served on active duty in Korea. Allard later moved to Paris, where he lived for several years, and then returned to the United States, where he taught French at several colleges.

While living in Boston, Massachusetts, Allard met author-illustrator James Marshall. The two collaborated on *The Stupids Step Out* (1974), and a fruitful relationship was born. Besides three further Stupids books, Allard and Marshall teamed up on numerous other books, including *It's So Nice to Have a Wolf Around the House* (1977), *Bumps in the Night* (1979), and the highly successful *Miss Nelson* books, about an eccentric grade school teacher.

With other illustrators, Allard has written such books as *May I Stay?* (1978), *The Hummingbird's Day* (1991), and *The Cactus Flower Bakery* (1991). Harry Allard continues to live and write in Massachusetts.

About the Illustrator of the *Stupids* Books

James Marshall (1942–1992)

One of the most beloved and original of contemporary children's book authors and illustrators, James Marshall was born on October 10, 1942, in San Antonio, Texas. His father was a farmer who also played in a band and worked on the railroad. Intending to become a musician, Marshall attended the New England Conservatory of Music in Boston, where he played the viola. However, an airplane accident caused a hand injury that ended his musical career.

Marshall returned to Texas and attended San Antonio College, later transferring to Southern Connecticut State University in New Haven, where he studied French and history. He began drawing by accident one summer day in 1971 while relaxing in a hammock. He soon became a children's book author and illustrator.

Besides the books he illustrated for Harry Allard, Marshall wrote and illustrated many books of his own, including his first, *George and Martha* (1972), about two lovelorn hippopotamuses; the *Fox* series of books; and *Goldilocks and the Three Bears* (1989), which earned him the Caldecott Honor citation in 1989. His illustrations are characterized by their childlike simplicity and outrageous sense of humor.

Marshall died unexpectedly of a brain tumor on October 13, 1992, at age fifty. In 2007, he was posthumously honored by the American Library Association with the Laura Ingalls Wilder Medal for his "substantial and lasting contribution to the literature for children."

Curses, Hexes & Spells (1974)
by Daniel Cohen

What Happens in *Curses, Hexes & Spells*

Part of the "Weird & Horrible Library" series, *Curses, Hexes & Spells* is a 1974 nonfiction book about colorful and legendary curses from history and folklore, cast on families, animals, specific places, and ghosts.

Challenges and Censorship

Author Daniel Cohen has called *Curses, Hexes & Spells* "a relatively lighthearted, simple, easy-to-read book which created no problems at all when it first came out. Over the years, as this fear of Satanism has grown among certain groups, this book has loomed larger."

The occult has always loomed large in Cohen's work. Many of his most popular books are about monsters, ghosts, and strange happenings. Why, then, have challengers in schools and libraries singled out this one title among all of Cohen's, making it seventy-third on the American Library Association's "100 Most Frequently Challenged Books of 1990–2000"? The author has no answers. "I really do not know why this rather nondescript book has gained this kind of notoriety," he said in an interview with author Herbert N. Foerstel.

One possible answer is that the book focuses on occult behavior that parents and other adults fear children will imitate. Fundamentalist Christians see *Curses, Hexes & Spells* not as a volume of information to educate readers about the occult, but rather as a how-to book to draw them into the dark arts of the occult. Cohen finds this ironic, since young-adult (YA) authors like himself are writing only to inform, not seduce. "Yet they [his books] are banned from schools, while children can go to the drug store and pick up books that pander to these beliefs," he says. "The kids are given no choice. They either get books that pander to occultism or they get nothing."

Interestingly, a 1990 article in the *New York Times* described *Curses, Hexes & Spells* as the fourth most frequently stolen book in the New York Public Library system.

Landmark Challenge:
Five Books on the Block in Howard County

Howard County, Maryland, schools were averaging five challenged books a year until the 1990–91 school year. That year, they had that many challenges before the end of the first semester. Besides *Curses, Hexes & Spells*, the challenged books included Susan Jeschke's *The Devil Did It* and C. S. Lewis's classic fantasy *The Lion, the Witch and the Wardrobe*.

Parents and residents who opposed the challenges outnumbered those who supported them. "If every interest group in Howard County starts requesting removal of materials which do not agree with its particular philosophy," read a petition signed by about 100 residents, "we could end up with a very diluted curriculum and reference library in our schools."

Celeste Smalkin, supervisor of the schools' media services, played down the number of challenges. "It's something that goes on all the time, especially at the elementary level," she explained. "The only thing that's been unusual is how much attention it has gotten."

The challenges were passed on to a Criteria Review Committee made up of six teachers, six parents and residents, and two students. The committee reviewed the challenges and books and unanimously rejected three of the challenges. *The Devil Did It*, a children's picture book in which a girl vanquishes a visiting demon with milk and cookies, was approved 11 to 2 by the committee. The vote displeased parent Lena Herlihy. "I strongly disagree with the idea that the devil is a friendly force," she said.

The most controversial book, however, was *Curses, Hexes & Spells*. While the committee voted 8 to 5 to retain it in the middle and high school libraries, it decided to have it removed from all elementary schools. While acknowledging it as a straightforward history of curses, hexes, and spells, Smalkin, who served on the committee, added, "We decided that it really could be misunderstood."

Landmark Challenge: Witchery Afoot in Wichita Falls

Curses, Hexes & Spells was just one of nine books with so-called "satanic" themes that Steve Lane, a parent of a student at Kirby Junior High School in Wichita Falls, Texas, wanted removed from that school's library and a neighboring high school's library in early 1997. He and thirty-four other members of the First Assembly of God Church requested that the school board trustees ban all nine. The four books from the Kirby library were in Lane's possession. Titles like *The Devil, Entertaining Satan,* and *Black Magic, White Magic* did not encourage the support of the trustees, although they insisted on hearing the recommendation of a challenge committee before making a final decision on the books' removal. Kirby Junior High librarian Nell Fonville claimed the books in question were purchased before she came to the school and would not have been bought by her.

Carrie Sperling, director of the North Texas Region of the American Civil Liberties Union (ACLU), called Fonville's lack of initiative in getting the books back on the shelves a violation of the First Amendment. "I think it's not only censorship, but it is illegal censorship," Sperling declared. "It seems to me [the books] are not being reviewed for their academic merits . . . but probably because certain public pressure groups disagree with what they have to say."

Further Reading

Buckley, Stephen. "Protests of Books on Rise; School Panel Reports Five Since September." *Washington Post*, December 20, 1990: m.01.

Foerstel, Herbert N. *Banned in the U.S.A.: A Reference Guide to Banned Books in Schools and Public Libraries.* Westport, Conn.: Greenwood Press, 2002.

Hamilton, John Maxwell. "Is There a Klepto in the Stacks?" *New York Times*, November 18, 1990: A1. Available online: http://query.nytimes. com/gst/fullpage.html?res=9C0CEED7103EF93BA25752C1A966 958260&sec=&spon=&partner=permalink&exprod=permalink. Accessed December 10, 2008.

"Wichita Falls, Texas." *Newsletter on Intellectual Freedom*, July 1987: 95.

About the Author of *Curses, Hexes & Spells*

Daniel Cohen (1936–   )

A prolific author of nonfiction books for young readers, Daniel Edward Cohen was born on March 12, 1936, in Chicago, Illinois. In 1958, he graduated from the University of Illinois at Urbana-Champaign with a degree in journalism. After a stint as a proofreader at Time, Inc., Cohen was hired as an editor for the periodical *Science Digest*. He left the publication in 1969 and moved with his wife to upstate New York to become a freelance writer.

Although Cohen has written about a wide range of topics, he is best known for his books on the occult, monsters, ghosts, and paranormal phenomena. A skeptic about these subjects, Cohen writes on them to inform and entertain, but neither endorses nor debunks. Among his more recent works are *Civil War Ghosts* (1999), *Yellow Journalism: Scandal, Sensationalism, and Gossip in the Media* (2000), and the *Discovering Dinosaurs* series (2000).

Cujo (1981)
by Stephen King

What Happens in *Cujo*

Set in the small town of Castle Rock, Maine, *Cujo* focuses on two families—the working-class Cambers and the upper-middle-class Trentons. Joe Camber is a mechanic who abuses his wife, Charity. Their family pet is a 200-pound Saint Bernard, Cujo, who one day is bitten on the nose by a rabid bat. Cujo gradually becomes rabid himself and is transformed from a gentle, friendly dog into a raving, murderous monster. The Trentons have problems of their own. Vic Trenton's ad business is failing and, with their marriage on the rocks, his wife, Donna, is having an affair. As Vic leaves on a business trip for Boston, Charity and her son, Brett, leave for a visit with her sister in Connecticut.

Cujo attacks and kills his first human victim, an alcoholic neighbor of the Camber family. When Joe investigates what has happened, he is also killed by Cujo. Donna, who has broken off her affair, drives to Joe's with her four-year-old son, Tad, to have their car fixed. The car breaks down in the Cambers' yard, and Cujo lays in wait for the mother and son to come out of the car. The two remain prisoners inside the car for three hellish days in the high heat of summer. During this time, the local sheriff shows up, but he is also killed by Cujo before he can call for help. In an attempt to get to the phone inside the Cambers' house, Donna is bitten twice by Cujo. Finally, Vic returns and comes to their rescue but is too late to save Tad, who dies from dehydration in the sweltering car.

Challenges and Censorship

It is a small irony that of all Stephen King's many horror novels, *Cujo*, which has virtually no supernatural elements, is the one most challenged in schools and libraries. It ranked fifty-fifth on the American Library Association's "100 Most Frequently Challenged Books of 1990–2000," putting it well above King's two other books on the list, *Carrie* (seventy-seventh place) and *The Dead Zone* (eighty-third place).

Unlike the other monsters and satanic creatures that populate King's work, Cujo is an ordinary dog who happens to become rabid. And this may explain the challenges: *Cujo*'s horrors are taken from real life and could happen to anyone. The family pet's transformation from friendly dog to vicious beast is one that could easily disturb both young and adult readers. Challengers have also focused on the use of profanity (common in all of King's novels), "degrading remarks made to women," graphic sex (including rape and masturbation), and the slow death of a young boy trapped in an overheated car.

King admitted in *On Writing* that he wrote the novel during an intense bout of alcohol and drug abuse and remembers little about its writing. *Cujo* was adapted into a movie in 1983, with Dee Wallace Stone starring as Donna Trenton and Danny Pintauro as her son, Tad.

Less involved in censorship cases of his work than some writers, King is nonetheless an outspoken critic of censorship. "Please remember that book-banning is censorship," he wrote in a letter to the *Bangor Daily News* in 1992, "and that censorship in a free society is always a serious matter . . . Book-banners, after all, insist that the entire community shall see things their way, and only their way."

Landmark Challenge:
Removing a "Bunch of Garbage" in Bradford

When it came to censoring *Cujo*, school officials in Bradford, New York, in 1985, went at it like a mad dog on the attack. "We didn't read the entire book, but there was no need to," said school board member Henry Bonarski. "We wanted it removed because it was a bunch of garbage."

The decision came after just five minutes of reading selected, premarked passages given to board members by their president after he discussed the book with the parents of an eighth-grader at the local middle school. One of the marked passages described the scorned lover of Donna Trenton, a main character in the book, masturbating on her bed. "I read one half of one paragraph," said board member Sandra Rogers, who brought the motion to ban the novel, "and I wouldn't read the rest of it."

The only issue board members were not in agreement on was whether *Cujo* should be permanently or only temporarily removed from school library shelves. The removal was temporary while a review and advisory committee was formed to look at all books found offensive by parents. "Red letter" books of particular concern would then be studied by the school board. "The committee will also review selection material that the librarian uses," explained Rogers. "We can't waste taxpayer money on mistakes like this one."

The current book policy states that parents can reject only materials used by their own children and not someone else's. It reads "to deny the freedom of choice in fear that it may be unwisely used is to destroy the freedom itself. The right of any individual not just to read but to read whatever he or she wants to read is basic to a democratic society."

Landmark Challenge:
A Librarian Caught in the Middle

The victims of a book challenge can vary widely—from the students denied the right to read a book to the teachers who can no longer teach it. In Berryville, Arkansas, it was a school librarian who suffered the most.

In 1988, Pamela Moore was in her second year as school librarian when her principal told her to remove *Cujo* from the shelves because he was "concerned about obscene language." The school superintendent intervened and told Moore to form a review committee. She did, and the committee recommended that the book remain in the library. A few days later, Moore was summoned to the superintendent's office for a meeting. Both the superintendent and the principal told her that if she followed the recommendation of the committee, "they would," in her words, "accept [her] resignation." Coerced by her bosses, Moore did not put *Cujo* back in the library. She would soon come to regret that decision.

The school board was divided over the banning of the book and seemed to hold Moore at least partially responsible. When offering her a new contract, they put restrictions on her position, leading her to finally resign. In 1991, she applied for unemployment benefits from the Department of Labor and was denied them. The Department of Labor claimed that "Moore's failure to attempt to resolve an unsatisfactory work situation through available channels, i.e., going to the school board with her concerns prior to quitting, precluded a determination of good cause."

Moore pled her case before the Arkansas Court of Appeals. On December 26, the court ruled in favor of the Department of Labor and dismissed her case on the grounds that she should have resisted the censorship more strongly. For Pamela Moore, the struggle over one library book was a no-win situation.

Landmark Challenge:
Trying to Change "A Double Standard" in Peru

Pat White's dissatisfaction with Stephen King's fiction began with *Cujo*, but it didn't stop there. When she made her formal complaint to a school committee at her son's junior-senior high school in Peru, Indiana, in late 1991, it was to remove a dozen of King's books from the school library.

"I believe, when the school provides this kind of filth for the children, the school is taking the responsibility out of the hands of the parents about what children read," she said. "We feel there's kind of a double standard here. You can't use that language in the hall, but you can pick up a book off the shelf and read it."

When the school committee decided the books would stay in the library, White took her challenge to the North Miami school board. The board heard the case on February 4, 1992, with Indianapolis attorney Robert Rund serving as a nonpartisan hearing officer.

The following month, Rund recommended that the board remove only three of the twelve King books—*Cujo*, *The Dead Zone* (1979), and *Christine* (1983). The board voted on Rund's recommendation on April 21. Before the final vote, superintendent of schools Stephen Wise put forth a motion that the three books be made available to students with parental permission, but no one would second the motion and it died.

The vote to ban was 5 to 1, with Vicki Deeds the sole board member opposing the ban. "I am an avid reader of all types of literature," she later said. "I have my favorite authors, although Stephen King is not one of them. If there are books in a library—public or school—that I do not approve of for literacy, style, or content, then I have the choice not to read such a book. But if other individuals want to read it, they also have the choice to do so. As a parent, I monitor the choice of material my children read, whether it's age or content appropriate. Other parents also have this responsibility."

Landmark Challenge: "De Facto Censorship" in Brooksville

Ann Carver's sixth-grade son thought the book he had borrowed from the West Hernando Middle School library in Brooksville, Florida, was another warm-hearted dog story like *Old Yeller*, one of his favorites. But he quickly discovered that *Cujo* was a far cry from *Old Yeller*. When he came to his mother to ask what certain swear words meant, she examined the book and found it inappropriate for her son or any other student under the age of sixteen. "I believe in freedom—whoever wants to may read that," Carver, a high school nurse, said in her September 1998 complaint. "But not a minor."

School principal Ken Pritz took the library's copy off the shelf to be passed around to the fourteen members of the review committee that would evaluate the book and make a recommendation. School media specialist Susan Vaughn had not read the book, but said it was a popular title that had been on the shelf since the school opened.

The committee reached its decision in October, recommending that *Cujo* be kept in a room in the library accessible only to teachers. Students could still check out *Cujo* with a signed permission slip from a parent, followed up by phone verification with a librarian. Vaughn was disappointed with the decision, which she called de facto censorship. The limited access meant that the book was virtually forgotten. "Experience shows that nobody checks it out," she said.

A second King book, *Different Seasons* (1982), a collection of novellas, or long stories, joined *Cujo* on the limited-access shelf in 2001 when a female student complained about a prison rape scene in the story *Rita Hayworth and Shawshank Redemption*. Vaughn said it was the first time in her twenty-one years as a school librarian that a child had challenged a book. "To teach kids that when someone is uncomfortable with material it's possible to get that material removed is a limiting of freedoms for all of us," she said.

Further Reading

Beahm, George, ed. *War of Words: The Censorship Debate*. Kansas City, Mo.: Andrews & McMeel, 1993.

"Bradford, New York." *Newsletter on Intellectual Freedom*, May 1985: 77–78.

Foerstel, Herbert N. *Banned in the U.S.A.: A Reference Guide to Book Censorship in Schools and Public Libraries*. Westport, Conn.: Greenwood Press, 2002.

Karolides, Nicholas J., Margaret Bald, and Dawn B. Sova. *120 Banned Books: Censorship Histories of World Literature*. New York: Facts On File, 2005.

King, Robert. "Parent Says Novel Too Sexually Explicit for Middle School Library." *St. Petersburg Times*, September 11, 1998: 1.

———. "School Limits King Book Access." *St. Petersburg Times*, October 2, 2001: 1.

"Little Rock, Arkansas." *Newsletter on Intellectual Freedom*, May 1992: 90.

"Peru, Indiana." *Newsletter on Intellectual Freedom*, May 1992: 80; July 1992: 106.

About the Author of *Cujo*

Stephen King (1947–   )

The undisputed king of horror fiction, Stephen King is one of the best-selling and most prolific authors of horror of all time. He was born in Portland, Maine, on September 21, 1947. His parents separated when he was still a child, and he and his older brother, David, lived in various places with their mother until settling permanently in Durham, Maine, when Stephen was eleven. After high school, King attended the University of Maine at Orono, where he wrote a weekly column for the campus paper and met his future wife, Tabitha. They married in 1971, a year after King graduated with a degree in English. They have three children.

King taught high school English at Hampden Academy in Hampden, Maine, for several years, writing stories in the evenings and on weekends. His first sales were to men's magazines. He nearly destroyed his first novel, *Carrie*, after numerous rejections, but was persuaded by his wife to keep trying to get it published. Doubleday finally accepted *Carrie* in 1973, and soon King was able to devote himself full time to writing.

He wrote *Salem's Lot* (1975), about vampires who take over a small town, in a room in his garage. Many novels followed, most of them set in his home state of Maine, where he still lives today. Among his many best-selling horror novels are *The Shining* (1977), *The Stand* (1978), *Pet Sematary* (1983), *It* (1986), *Misery* (1987), *Dolores Claiborne* (1993), *The Green Mile* (1996), *Cell* (2006), and *Lisey's Story* (2006). Most of these, as well as many other works, have been adapted into films and television movies. King has also written six volumes of collected short stories and seven novels under the pseudonym Richard Bachman. His nonfiction works include *Danse Macabre* (1981), a personal survey of horror in literature and other media, and *On Writing: A Memoir of the Craft* (2000).

Stephen King was struck by a car and seriously injured while walking on a road near his home in Maine on June 19, 1999. He has since fully recovered. King was the 2003 recipient of the National Book Foundation's Medal for Distinguished Contribution to American Letters.

A Light in the Attic (1981)
by Shel Silverstein

What Happens in *A Light in the Attic*

This collection of verse contains 136 whimsical poems for children illustrated with author Shel Silverstein's distinctive black-and-white line drawings. Among the most memorable and controversial of the poems are those that dole out naughty and cautionary advice for children. In "How Not to Have to Dry the Dishes," the reader is taught that breaking a dish or two is a sure way not to be asked to do this chore again. In "Prayer of the Selfish Child," the child prays that if he should die "before I wake," the Lord will break all his toys so other children can't play with them.

Life in Silverstein's strange world is often fraught with danger and death. In "The Sitter," a babysitter actually sits on her charges, while an anteater in the poem of that name is really an "aunt" eater. "Snap!" is about an umbrella that eats people, and in "Fancy Dive," Melissa of Coconut Grove does a perfect dive into a swimming pool that she only realizes too late has no water.

Sometimes the title promises the nonsense to come, as with "The Meehoo with an Exactly Watt" (a takeoff on the famous Abbott and Costello routine "Who's on First?"), "Who Ordered the Broiled Face?" and "Unscratchable Itch." As the author advises in one poem: "Put something silly in the world/That ain't been there before."

Challenges and Censorship

When it appeared in 1981, Shel Silverstein's *A Light in the Attic* became a publishing phenomenon. This book of poetry, aimed at children but enjoyed equally by adults, remained on the *New York Times* best-seller list for 182 weeks—a record at that time—and sold more than one million copies by 1985. "Mr. Silverstein's work remains a must for lovers of good verse for children," wrote X. J. Kennedy in his review of the book in the *Times*. "Quite like nobody else, he is still a master of delectable outrage and the 'proprietor' of a surprisingly finely tuned sensibility."

But it was the outrageousness of Silverstein's poetry and not its sensibility that disturbed many parents and administrators who challenged it in classrooms and school libraries. The reasons for the challenges are many. One parent declared that twenty-four of the book's poems were not suitable for children. Another challenger accused Silverstein of "glorifying Satan, suicide, and cannibalism."

The poems are filled with enough macabre happenings and grisly deaths to disturb some adults, although most children delight in them. In "Ticklish Tom," the boy of the title rolls in his tickled state onto railroad tracks. "Rumble, rumble, whistle, roar," goes the poem, "Tom ain't ticklish anymore." Other poems flirt with the scatological (references to bodily functions). In "Quick Trip," two children are swallowed by a monster called a Gink and are then defecated out his rear end still alive. In "Spelling Bee," the narrator is stung on her naked behind by a literate bee who writes in bee stings, "Hello . . . You've Been Stung By A Bee," all of which is fully illustrated.

A Light in the Attic ranked fifty-first on the American Library Association's "100 Most Frequently Challenged Books of 1990–2000." It holds the added distinction of being one of only two books of poetry to make that infamous list. The other is Eve Merriam's *Halloween ABC*.

Landmark Challenge:
Little Abigail and the Unpleasant Challenge

Few poems in *A Light in the Attic* have raised more challenges than "Little Abigail and the Beautiful Pony." It is both one of the book's wittiest verses and one of its most controversial. "I was just outraged by it all," said Sherry Towne, a parent of a student at the Fruitland Park Elementary School in Fruitland Park, Florida. "It teaches children to manipulate their parents." When Abigail is denied the pony by her parents, she cries, "If I don't get that pony

I'll die." And she takes to her bed and does just that. In an afterword, the author urges kids to tell the story to their own parents when they won't buy them something.

In response to Towne's 2003 challenge, the school formed a review committee made up of parents and teachers. They voted not only to reject the challenge and keep the book on library shelves, but also requested that the school develop a lesson in the curriculum dealing with nonsensical poetry. Unhappy with this decision, Towne appealed to a school district committee, which only endorsed the review committee's recommendation. In her reaction, Towne insisted, "We cram this crap down our children's throats. We have a responsibility for raising our children." Although she threatened to appeal again, Sherry Towne failed to do so.

"Youngsters obviously have a better understanding of the difference between fact and fiction than Towne is willing to give them credit for," wrote Sam Fenton, editor of the *Orlando Sentinel*'s Lake County section, in an editorial.

In a previous challenge to the poem in Huffman, Texas, in 1989, the focus was placed not on manipulating parents but on suicide. "I think it's sick," said Barbara McGaugh, referring to the girl's willful death. "It plants the seed. We're trying to keep suicide out of our schools, not in them." Douglass Shands, superintendent of schools in the Huffman Independent School District, called the book "disturbing to young minds" and banned it from classrooms. He might have had a better understanding of Silverstein's intentions if he had sat in on the nonsensical poetry session at Fruitland Park Elementary School.

Further Reading

Becker, Beverly C., and Susan M. Stans. *Hit List for Children 2: Frequently Challenged Books*. Chicago: American Library Association, 2002.

Honan, William H. "Shel Silverstein, Zany Writer and Cartoonist, Dies at 67." *New York Times*, May 11, 1999: B10.

Kennedy, X. J. "A Rhyme Is a Chime." *New York Times*, November 15, 1981: A51.

McDowell, Edwin. "'A Light In The Attic' Sets Best Seller Record." *New York Times*, January 10, 1985: C16.

Mercier, Jean F. "Shel Silverstein: An Interview by *Publisher's Weekly*." Shel Silverstein Archive, February 24, 1975. Available online:

http://members.tripod.com/~ShelSilverstein/ShelPW.html. Accessed December 17, 2007.

Zammarelli, Chris. "All Because of a Pony Her Parents Wouldn't Buy." Bookslut.com, February 2004. Available online: www.bookslut.com/banned_bookslut/2004_02_001498.php. Accessed December 14, 2007.

About the Author of *A Light in the Attic*

Shel Silverstein (1930–1999)

A wildly imaginative author whose talents spanned children's books, stage plays, and hit songs, Shel Silverstein was truly a Renaissance man of letters. He was born Sheldon Alan Silverstein on September 25, 1930, in Chicago, Illinois. In his early twenties, he joined the U.S. Army and was stationed in Japan and Korea in the 1950s. While in Asia, he became a cartoonist for the Pacific edition of the military newspaper *Stars and Stripes*. His first published book was *Grab Your Socks!* (1956), a collection of his cartoons for that publication.

Silverstein was not immediately drawn to writing for children. His *Uncle Shelby's ABZ Book* (1961) was actually a wicked parody of a children's book. But soon after, a friend and an editor convinced him to try his hand at writing for children. One of his first efforts, *The Giving Tree* (1964), was a touching fable that, like many of his works, contained his own eloquent but simple illustrations. It sold more than 100,000 copies in a single year. Similarly popular were Silverstein's first two poetry collections for children, *Where the Sidewalk Ends* (1974) and *A Light in the Attic* (1981). Silverstein's imagination was often dark and gruesome, but made palatable for children by his impish sense of humor.

In addition to his children's books, Silverstein wrote nine plays for adults and co-wrote the screenplay for the black comedy *Things Change* (1988), directed by playwright David Mamet.

Among his many hit songs were such novelty classics as "A Boy Named Sue" (Johnny Cash), "The Unicorn" (the Irish Rovers), and "Cover of the Rolling Stone" (Dr. Hook and the Medicine Show). He also recorded many albums of his songs and music. Silverstein was inducted posthumously into the Nashville Songwriters Hall of Fame in 2002.

A free spirit, Silverstein divided his time between a houseboat in Sausalito, California, and homes in Martha's Vineyard, Massachusetts; Greenwich Village, New York City; and Key West, Florida. He died of a heart attack in Key West sometime during the weekend of May 8–9, 1999. His last book, published after his death, was *Runny Babbit: A Billy Sook*, a collection of nonsense poems filled with spoonerisms, pairs of words that have the first letters exchanged.

"I would hope that people, no matter what age, would find something to identify with in my books, pick one up and experience a personal sense of discovery," Silverstein said in a 1975 interview, one of the last he ever gave. "That's great. But for them, not for me. I think if you're a creative person, you should just go about your business, do your work and not care about how it's received."

The Witches (1983)
by Roald Dahl

What Happens in *The Witches*

After the seven-year-old narrator of the novel suffers the loss of his parents in a car accident, he goes to live with his grandmother in Norway. The grandmother is an eccentric but loving old woman who smokes cigars and tells her grandson all about witches. Contrary to legend, she explains to him, modern witches live like ordinary people but have a great aversion to all children. Soon after, the boy and his grandmother, now his guardian, return to live in England, as set down in the provisions of his parents' will.

The grandmother plans a summer vacation in Norway, but ill health forces them to change their plans. Instead, they stay at a seaside hotel in Bournemouth, England. The boy has two pet mice that he keeps hidden from the hotel staff and takes to a banquet room to train in secret. While there, the members of the Royal Society for the Prevention of Cruelty to Children enter the room for their annual meeting.

As the boy watches from his hiding place, he is horrified to discover that these ordinary-looking women are actually the witches of England, led by their leader, the terrible Grand High Witch. The Grand High Witch has concocted a diabolical plot to rid England of all children by turning them into mice by means of a special Delayed Action Mouse-Maker formula poured over candy. When the children arrive at school the following morning, they will be exterminated by teachers and school staff, who won't realize the mice are their pupils. To demonstrate the power of her formula, the Grand

High Witch turns an unsuspecting boy, Bruno Jenkins, into a mouse before the narrator's eyes.

Before he can escape, the witches discover the narrator, and he, too, is turned into a mouse. He manages to escape from the witches and leads Bruno back to his grandmother's room. Accepting his fate, the boy/mouse plans with his grandmother to stop the witches by dousing their own food with the Delayed Action Mouse-Maker, which he steals from the room of the Grand High Witch. Bruno is more interested in eating than helping with the scheme.

That night, the boy/mouse slips into the kitchen and pours all the Mouse-Maker into the tureen that contains the soup the witches will eat for dinner. They all drink the soup, are transformed into mice, and are promptly killed by the horrified hotel staff.

Leaving Bruno with his parents, the boy/mouse and his grandmother return to Norway. She tells him that the new Grand High Witch lives in a castle in Norway. With her help, he plans to slip into her castle and give her a dose of the Mouse-Maker, which the two will concoct themselves. Then he will go through her records and discover the names of all the witches in each country of the world. He and his grandmother will spend the remaining days of their lives hunting down and destroying all the remaining witches. "I can't wait to get started!" cries the grandmother as the book ends.

Challenges and Censorship

"REAL WITCHES dress in ordinary clothes and look very much like ordinary women," writes Roald Dahl in "A Note About Witches," which opens his novel. "They live in ordinary homes and they work in ORDINARY JOBS. That is why they are so hard to catch."

It is this intrusion of these legendary hags into the modern, everyday world that makes *The Witches* so fascinating and, for some readers, so disturbing. Like other children's books by Dahl, it has become a modern classic. "It is a curious sort of tale but an honest one, which deals with matters of crucial importance to children: smallness, the existence of evil in the world, mourning, separation, death," wrote novelist Erica Jong in her *New York Times* review in 1983. In a review of a 1994 biography of Roald Dahl, horror writer Stephen King called *The Witches* and other works by Dahl for children "good-hearted books, for the most part, filled with optimism and good cheer (as well as the occasional stab of beastliness)."

"Down with children!" gleefully sings the Grand High Witch, a truly terrifying creature. "Do them in!/Boil their bones and fry their skin!/Bish them, squish them, bash them, mash them!/Brrreak them, shake them, slash them, smash them!" Such violence aimed at children by these horrific creatures may delight many children who revel in fantasy, but not all of their parents are delighted. Dahl's characteristic droll humor and gruesome imagination have brought plenty of school challenges over the years.

Another cause for concern has been the fate of the poor narrator, who is turned into a mouse—and unlike many of the protagonists of more traditional fairy tales, is never turned back into a boy. He revels in his mousehood and is not even disturbed much when his beloved grandmother tells him he will live, at the most, another nine years. "It doesn't matter who you are or what you look like," he says, "so long as somebody loves you."

For these reasons, *The Witches* has been Dahl's most challenged book, ranking twenty-seventh on the American Library Association's "100 Most Frequently Challenged Books of 1990–2000."

The Witches was adapted into a movie in 1990, directed by Nicolas Roeg and starring Anjelica Huston as the Grand High Witch. While many critics considered the film one of the best adaptations of Dahl's work, the author himself hated it.

Landmark Challenge:
Repelled by Two "Revolting" Books in Iowa

Denise Zirkelbach, mother of a child at a local elementary school in Maquoketa, Iowa, found Roald Dahl's book of children's verse *Revolting Rhymes* truly revolting, but she devoted most of her November 1989 written complaint to criticizing *The Witches*. The book should be removed from the school library, Zirkelbach argued, for its violence, the subject of witches, and the grim fact that "the boy who is turned into a mouse by the witches will have to stay a mouse for the rest of his life."

The school's principal made it clear that he was against censorship, but added, "I don't consider removing these two books censorship." He insisted, however, that the school's policy would be adhered to and that the books would remain available to students in the library while a Reconsideration Committee examined the challenge and made its recommendation.

Public opinion over the challenge was divided. The Maquoketa Public Library's head librarian supported keeping *The Witches* but not *Revolting Rhymes*, which she intended to remove from her own library. When public library board members read it, however, they expressed their fondness for the book, and she kept it in the collection.

On January 2, 1990, the Reconsideration Committee met in closed session and decided that both of Dahl's books met all the criteria for library selection. They voted to keep the books in all district elementary libraries and curriculum.

Landmark Challenge:
Laying Down the Law in Dallas, Oregon

Parent Vicki Shones's challenge in spring 1991 at Rickreall Elementary School in Dallas, Oregon, was a unique one. Shones held that *The Witches* violated a state statute, or law, that required public schools to teach ethics and morality and "other lessons which tend to promote and develop an upright and desirable citizenry."

For Shones, there was nothing moral or upright about *The Witches*, which she charged was gruesome, violent, and perhaps likely to lead impressionable young readers to experiment with witchcraft. A review committee considered the challenge and recommended retaining the book in a vote of 11 to 2. In an August meeting, the school board agreed with the recommendation, but it did put restrictions on classroom use of another book about the occult, the nonfiction *Visions of the Future: Magic Boards*, by Saul Stadtmauer.

Shones accepted her defeat but still felt the law was not being upheld by school officials. "It's not my intent to censor what's available," she said. "But we have a positive law that addresses this subject and just because it may not be popular, we don't use it. I don't think that's any option here."

Landmark Challenge: Broaching "Common
Decency" in Escondido, California

The four parents from the Escondido Union School District who filed official complaints against *The Witches* in December 1991 had plenty to complain about. "We object to the introduction to the occult, to the teaching about witchcraft that this book claims to be fact, to the parts about cutting kids up, destroying them, and making them disappear," wrote one of the parents. For another parent, Carla Grabianowski, the book would only lead to "desensitization to violence, increased interest in the practice of witchcraft, the learning of unhealthy ways in dealing with differing groups of people."

Assistant superintendent Jim Fitzpatrick agreed with the challengers. "It [*The Witches*] was offensive in terms of common decency standards," he said. He felt so strongly about the issue that when a review committee recommended in a 3 to 1 vote that the book be retained, he and superintendent Bob Fisher overrode the recommendation. In February 1992, Fitzpatrick ordered the book be placed on a reserve shelf in the school library, requiring any students from kindergarten through fifth grade to submit written parental permission to borrow it. *The Witches* became the first library book to ever be restricted in the Escondido Union School District. It wasn't the occult influence, Fitzpatrick claimed, that led to his decision, but the fear that "youngsters at a primary age would become frightened."

Another elementary school principal and review committee member, Stan Reid, disagreed with this assessment. "It was a tongue-in-cheek approach and the bottom line was that good will overcome evil," he said. "In talking with kids out in the playground and in the lunch lines, for the most part the kids thought it was hilarious. They understood that it was a fairy tale and it was make believe."

Angry with Fisher's decision, the district school board instructed staff members to draw up a new policy that would give the board, not the superintendent, the power to restrict library books. The new policy required that book review committees composed of six parents and six school employees be formed to deal with book challenges.

In early June 1993, the school board voted to take the novel off the restricted list and put it back on the regular library shelves. "We now have a framework in place to handle these complaints that seems to work," said district office employee Bill Simpson.

Although *The Witches* was available once again to students, four books remained on the library's banned list, including Eve Merriam's *Halloween ABC*, which was accused of the same charge leveled earlier against Dahl's book—promoting the occult.

Further Reading

Becker, Beverly C., and Susan M. Stans. *Hit List for Children 2: Frequently Challenged Books*. Chicago: American Library Association, 2002.

"Dallas, Oregon." *Newsletter on Intellectual Freedom*, January 1992: 26–27.

"Escondido, California." *Newsletter on Intellectual Freedom*, May 1992: 78–79.

Foerstel, Herbert N. *Banned in the U.S.A.: A Reference Guide to Book Censorship in Schools and Public Libraries*. Westport, Conn.: Greenwood Press, 2002.

Jong, Erica. "The Boy Who Became A Mouse." *New York Times*, November 13, 1983: A45. Available online: http://query.nytimes.com/gst/fullpage.html?res=9805EFDE1239F930A25752C1A965948260&sec=&spon=&partner=permalink&exprod=permalink. Accessed December 10, 2007.

King, Stephen. "The Fantastic Mr. Dahl." *Washington Post*, April 10, 1994: x.01.

"Maquoketa, Iowa." *Newsletter on Intellectual Freedom*, May 1990: 105–106.

McDonald, Kathy. "School District to Get Book Policy." *Los Angeles Times*, May 28, 1992: 8.

About the Author of *The Witches*

See biography in *James and the Giant Peach* entry.

The *Scary Stories* Books (1981–1991)
by Alvin Schwartz

What Happens in the *Scary Stories* Books

Scary Stories is a series of three books with frightful tales drawn from folklore and urban legends, researched and adapted by Alvin Schwartz. The first volume, *Scary Stories to Tell in the Dark*, appeared in 1981, and was followed by *More Scary Stories to Tell in the Dark* (1984), and *Scary Stories 3: More Tales to Chill Your Bones* (1991). Each book is divided into chapters that contain stories with a theme, such as ghosts, scary things, and humorous horror stories. They also include songs and poetry. One chapter in the first book is entitled "Aaaaaaaaaaah!" and contains "jump stories," which end with an expected scare to make the listener jump with fright.

While many of the stories focus on the supernatural, some have no ghosts or monsters. For example, "High Beams" is about a girl driving home who appears to be terrorized by a truck driver who keeps putting his high beams on from behind and follows her closely. When she finally stops and the police arrive, the reader learns that the truck driver was trying to protect her from a man in the back seat of her car who had a knife and was threatening to stab her.

In "Aaron Kelly's Bones," the horrors lend themselves to humor. The dead man of the title returns home to his wife, who resents his rotting corpse. She invites her new boyfriend, a fiddler, to come over. He plays his fiddle, encouraging Aaron to dance. The corpse dances so vigorously that his bones eventually fall apart.

The ghoulishness of the stories is perfectly matched by the grotesque illustrations by Stephen Gammell. Each book ends with an extensive bibliography, scholarly notes, and source information showing the origins of each tale.

Challenges and Censorship

Alvin Schwartz's trilogy of *Scary Stories* books has the distinction of being number one on the American Library Association's "100 Most Frequently Challenged Books of 1990–2000." On the People for the American Way's "America's Most Censored List" for 1994–95, *More Scary Stories* ranked first, *Scary Stories* second, and *Scary Stories 3* came in sixth place. The series continues its reign of terror in the new century, placing sixth on the ALA's "10 Most Frequently Challenged Books of 2001" for "occult/Satanism, unsuited to age group, violence and insensitivity."

So what makes these scary stories so scary that they have parents and other adults challenging them at an alarming rate? The gruesome tales, all taken from real folklore and urban legends, are indeed gruesome. For example, in the first volume's "The Haunted House," a preacher is confronted by the ghost of a young woman. "Her hair was torn and tangled, and the flesh was dropping off her face so he could see the bones and part of her teeth," Schwartz writes. "She had no eyeballs, but there was a sort of blue light way back in her eye sockets. And she had no nose to her face." Stephen Gammell's accompanying portrait of this hideous creature is more ghastly than Schwartz's description. Indeed, Gammell's unsettling drawings are a main reason for the books' controversial position and have been noted in a number of challenges. In another dark tale, "Wonderful Sausages," from *More Scary Stories*, a butcher murders his wife and grinds her up to make a "special sausage" that he sells to his unsuspecting customers.

While parents and school officials have found these stories too frightening for children, children, for the most part, have found them irresistible. The simple, straightforward way Schwartz tells them (none are longer than a few pages in length) lends the stories to being read aloud, like scary stories told around a campfire. In fact, in the first book's acknowledgments, the author thanks "the Boy Scouts at Camp Roosevelt at East Eddington, Maine, who told me their scary stories."

The *Scary Stories* books aren't the only Schwartz works to be challenged. *Cross Your Fingers, Spit in Your Hat*, a book of folk superstitions, ranked fiftieth on the ALA's "100 Most Frequently Challenged Books of 1990–2000." Another Schwartz book, *Telling Fortunes*, was challenged by an evangelical preacher in Rockdale County, Georgia, in 1998. "The book is evil," declared the Rev. Stephen Pentecost before the Rockdale County school board. "You don't put guns in kids' hands, you don't put alcohol in kids' hands, you don't put pornography in kids' hands, and you don't put this in their hands either . . . There are enough negative influences out there already, we don't need this one."

Landmark Challenge: Awakening a Sleeping Giant in Lakewood, Colorado

Parents in Lakewood, Colorado, attempted to get rid of Alvin Schwartz's *In a Dark, Dark Room and Other Scary Stories* (an I Can Read book published by Harper) twice, but school officials resisted their efforts both times. "I'm disappointed, of course," said one of the challengers after the first attempt was rejected in May 1986 by a committee composed of teachers, administrators, and parents. "But in the position school officials are in they can't be pressured by parents' groups. They feel they can't let parents tell them what to do. That's unfortunate. It won't make us quit, though. We'll appeal and we don't get tired. We'll take this as far as it will go. And we'll be back looking at more books in the fall, and hopefully more parents will be looking with us."

After losing the challenge against Schwartz's book, the parents lost again when challenging three more books in the curriculum at Lakewood High School—*Literature of the Supernatural*, *Monsters*, and *Topics for the Restless*. They had accused the books of promoting sexual promiscuity and the occult and of attacking American values.

"This is the first time in the ten years I've been teaching the class [on the supernatural] that it's been challenged," said Lakewood High English teacher Ann Klaiman. "I've had more parents ask me how I can justify teaching John Steinbeck." She did feel, however, that the challenges were part of "the forces of democracy," and that it is "certainly better than having the parents not care at all what their kids read."

The parents regrouped and took their challenge against all four books directly to the Jefferson County school board. On June 19, the board upheld the earlier decision by the review committee and superintendent John Peper that the books should be retained. "If a child can't be exposed to other points of view and rely on his parents to correct them if they're wrong, then he's in trouble," said board member Glen Keller. "I would be offended by a library that I could walk through and not find some book that offended me," said Kirk Brady, another board member.

The challenging parents were discouraged but were not about to give up. They vowed to return the following fall to make new challenges. "It's one thing to oppose a group of radicals and another thing to oppose concerned parents," said Lynn Miller, father of a student. "They've awakened a sleeping giant."

Landmark Challenge:
The "Stuff of Nightmares" in Enfield, Connecticut

"I'm not looking for censorship," insisted J. Daniel Merlino to school officials in Enfield, Connecticut. "I'm just looking for standards." Merlino was protesting teachers' reading aloud in class from the *Scary Stories* books to his third-grade son and first-grade daughter. "I can appreciate the creativity," Merlino stated in his 1994 challenge. "But the images in these books are surreal. A throat being torn out. A liver being eaten. These images are the stuff of nightmares."

Merlino's complaint was taken up by the school's Controversial Material Committee and denied. Fifth-grade teacher Mary Lombardo, who headed the committee, saw the stories and other horror fiction as high-interest reading materials for many students who might otherwise be reluctant to read.

Merlino persisted in his challenge, however, and a year later took it directly to the school board. At a February 1995 meeting, he and his wife, Linda, submitted a petition signed by sixty residents, asking that not only Schwartz's books, but all horror books, be removed from school libraries. The couple also presented to the board a letter from child therapist Cynthia Porter, who felt that reading Schwartz's horror tales could seriously traumatize children.

Other parents and teachers spoke in the books' defense. "I just feel that what my child reads is my decision and I want the books in the school library," said Parent-Teacher Organization (PTO) president Julie Sanchez. "The scariest part is actually the desire to censor these books," said elementary school librarian James Bowman.

Several weeks later, the board reconvened to vote on the issue. Board members were just as divided as other members of the community. Board member W. Franklin Wood declared that the books have "zero educational value" and accused school librarians of showing poor judgment in buying them for the schools. "It is much more dangerous as a society to screen and censor," countered board member Nelson Gamage. "Intellectual freedom must be preserved."

Board members came up with proposal after proposal to resolve the issue. One was to restrict the books to students in fifth grade and up. Another was to ban teachers from reading the *Scary Stories* books aloud in elementary classrooms. None passed. The meeting seemed deadlocked until superintendent John Gallacher came up with a compromise. He recommended keeping the books in the school libraries but restricting them to fourth-grade and up. Any younger student who wanted to borrow one of the books would need written permission from a parent. The proposal passed 6 to 2. While some saw the compromise as a workable solution, others lamented it. "I think it's censorship," said Bowman, "It's sad."

Landmark Challenge: "Imprisoned by Fear" in Louisville

Beth Dorsey's granddaughter was too young to read the stories in *Scary Stories 3*, a book given to her by a friend at school in March 2006, but the pictures alone so terrified her that she was "plagued by nightmares" and for months was "imprisoned by fear."

Dorsey told the Greater Clark County school board in Louisville, Kentucky, that she wanted all three volumes of Alvin Schwartz's gruesome series banned from Utica Elementary School's library for depicting—both verbally and pictorially—cannibalism, murder, witchcraft, and a person being skinned alive.

A review committee composed of teachers, parents, and residents was set up to evaluate the complaint. It rejected the challenge, saying that the book was appropriate for older elementary students. Dorsey, who had a petition signed by 175 residents who supported her challenge, appealed her case to superintendent of schools Thomas Rohr. Rohr backed the committee's recommendation and urged the school board to do the same. On August 8, the Greater Clark County school board met and voted 7 to 0 to reject Dorsey's request, stressing that the books had been on the library's shelves for years. "How could this have happened?" responded Beth Dorsey on hearing the decision. "I can't believe it."

Further Reading

Becker, Beverly C., and Susan M. Stans. *Hit List for Children 2: Frequently Challenged Books*. Chicago: American Library Association, 2002.

"Bozeman, Montana." *Newsletter on Intellectual Freedom*, September 1994: 166.

"Lakewood, Colorado." *Newsletter on Intellectual Freedom*, September 1986: 173; November 1986: 224–225.

Lambert, Bruce. "Alvin Schwartz, 64, an Author of Folklore Books for Children." *New York Times*, March 16, 1992: B8. Available online: http://query.nytimes.com/gst/fullpage.html?res=9E0CE6D6153B F935A25750C0A964958260&sec=&spon=&partner=permalink& exprod=permalink. Accessed December 10, 2007.

"Louisville, Kentucky." *Newsletter on Intellectual Freedom*, November 2006: 317–318. Available online: https://members.ala.org/nif/v55n6/ success_stories.html. Accessed December 10, 2007.

O'Neill, Helen. "Board Takes on Issue of Gory Books." *Hartford Courant*, February 10, 1995: B1.

———. "For Some, 'Scary Stories' in Schools Go Beyond Deviltry." *Hartford Courant*, January 21, 1995: A1.

———. "School Board Votes 6-2 to Limit Access to Controversial Series of 'Scary Stories.' *Hartford Courant*, March 1, 1995: B5.

About the Author of the *Scary Stories* Books

Alvin Schwartz (1927–1992)

Alvin Schwartz scared and entertained young readers with his numerous books on folklore, native wit, and superstitions for more than three decades. He was born on April 25, 1927, in Brooklyn, New York, where his father drove a taxi. When he was about eleven years old, Alvin created his own newspaper about his large extended family, filled with news and tasty gossip. He earned a bachelor's degree from Colby College in Maine in 1949 and a master's degree in journalism from Northwestern University in Chicago in 1951. For the next twelve years, he worked as a newspaper reporter and editor in upstate New York, before becoming a full-time freelance writer in 1963.

Schwartz's first children's work, *The Night Workers* (1966), was a nonfiction book about people who work at night. More nonfiction books followed until he discovered the delights of American folklore with *Tongue Twisters* (1972), which became a best-selling book. "My feeling was, my goodness, if this is the response, I certainly must pursue this!" Schwartz said. "And that's what happened."

Dozens of books on many aspects of folklore followed, all of them assiduously researched. They included *Witcracks: Jokes and Jests from American Folklore* (1973), *Cross Your Fingers, Spit in Your Hat: Superstitions and Other Beliefs* (1974), and *Flapdoodle: Pure Nonsense from American Folklore* (1980).

In 1981, Schwartz wrote the first of his three enormously popular *Scary Stories* books. The last of his more than fifty books was *And the Green Grass Grew All Around* (1992), a collection of folk poetry. Schwartz lived with his wife in Princeton, New Jersey. He died of lymphoma on March 14, 1992, at the age of sixty-four.

About the Illustrator of the *Scary Stories* Books

Stephen Gammell (1943–   )

A prominent illustrator of children's books, Stephen Gammell was born on February 10, 1943, and raised in Des Moines, Iowa. His father was the art editor for several national magazines and encouraged Stephen's gift for drawing. Completely self-taught, Gammell began his career as a commercial freelance artist.

He published his first children's book, *A Nutty Business*, with text by Ida Chittum, in 1973. Since then, he has illustrated more than fifty books. They include two Caldecott Honor books—*Where the Buffaloes Begin* (1982) and *The Relatives Came* (1986)—and the Caldecott Medal winner, *Song and Dance Man* (1988). Among his most recent books are *Humble Pie* (2002), *Timothy Cox Will Not Change His Socks* (2005), and *The Secret Science Project That Almost Ate the School* (2006).

"I try to have that element of surprise and fun in every drawing," Gammell once said. "This is why I never do any sketches beforehand, or plan ahead. My desire is that it happens for me in much the same way it happens to whoever will be looking at the book."

Gammell lives in St. Paul, Minnesota, with his wife, Linda, a photographer.

The *Goosebumps* Books (1992–1997)
by R. L. Stine

What Happens in the *Goosebumps* Books

A young-adult (YA) horror novel series consisting of sixty-two titles, *Goosebumps* deals with real-life contemporary teenagers in scary encounters with monsters, ghosts, and aliens, but usually with a good lacing of humor.

One of the most popular *Goosebumps* books and typical of the series is *The Haunted Mask*. In it, a young girl wears a horror mask for Halloween trick-or-treating and later learns that she can't take it off. She soon begins to behave like the hideous monster of the mask. In *Night of the Living Dummy*, the best-selling *Goosebumps* book, ventriloquist dummies come to life and wreak havoc. The book was so popular it spawned two sequels.

While a number of the book titles, such as *Night of the Living Dummy*, are take-offs on horror film titles (*Night of the Living Dead*), other books are parodies of classic films, such as *The Phantom of the Auditorium* (inspired by *The Phantom of the Opera*).

While there is gore in the books, it never gets too graphic, and the horror is leavened by plenty of humor. The first book in the original series was *Welcome to Dead House* (1992); the last was *Monster Blood V* (1997). Author R. L. Stine has also written two spin-off series, *Give Yourself Goosebumps* (1995), with a choose-your-own-ending format, and *Goosebumps: Series 2000* (1998–   ).

Challenges and Censorship

"I wanted *Goosebumps* to have the same kind of feeling you get on a roller-coaster ride," R. L. Stine once said about his horror novel series. "Lots of thrills . . . Lot of wild twists and turns. And a feeling of being safe the whole time."

The formula has worked incredibly well—young readers have gotten back on Stine's roller coaster time after time. To date, the sixty-two original *Goosebumps* titles have sold more than 300 million copies worldwide and have been translated into twenty-eight languages. The series has spawned spin-offs, direct-to-video movies, a television series, board games, video games, and T-shirts.

Hardly the kind of literature that is put on middle or high school reading lists, the paperbacks are still extremely popular in school and public libraries. Many teachers and parents see the books in a positive light because they motivate children to read. "At that age [her son is eight], they start reading a book, but you have to make them finish it," said Margit Hoffman of Thousand Oaks, California. "And these books really keep them motivated to read them through to the end." "Horror is a big thing in the house," said Debi Blum of Heardon, Virginia, whose twelve-year-old daughter loves *Goosebumps* and other YA horror books. "I don't think it affects them. If they started doing bizarre things, maybe I'd start looking at the books."

But other parents disagree. "The violence, the gory stuff, does it desensitize them?" asked Elizabeth Wooten of Fairfax, Virginia. "I think it does. I truly believe in the power of evil, and I've said to Katie [her daughter], it's not worth inviting those forces into your life." These beliefs have led to many challenges from parents and administrators, lifting *Goosebumps* to sixteenth place on the American Library Association's "100 Most Frequently Challenged Books of 1990–2000." The series was number one on the ALA's "10 Most Frequently Challenged Books of 1996." Most of the challenges have focused on satanic and occult elements, violence, and graphic horror.

The challenges and censorship don't seem to bother Stine. "I'm proud and humble," he said in an interview with CNN in 1999. "I think it's more a sign of success. My feeling is that anything that becomes really popular in this country is going to be attacked by some people. It's just the price you pay for being popular."

Landmark Challenge:
The Nightmare That Sparked a Challenge

When a fourth-grader at Maine School in Parks, Arizona, woke up from a nightmare in late 1996, the superintendent of schools took it seriously. The boy, according to his parents, had just read a *Goosebumps* book borrowed from the school library. The horror novel, they believed, had caused the bad dream.

The superintendent took immediate action. He ordered all copies of *Goosebumps* books removed from the school library. The school's parent-teacher organization was not pleased by this act of censorship. The superintendent modified his stance and ordered the books returned to the library shelves, but under restrictions. A special message that went home to parents soon after read: "*Goosebumps* books may only be checked out by third, fourth, fifth, and sixth grade students. *Fear Street* books [another horror series by R. L. Stine] may only be checked out by sixth grade students. If you wish that your child not read any of these books, please let the school know."

When this message came to the attention of former school board member Zane Morris, he was incensed. At a December 10 meeting of the board, he pointedly asked board members, "What right do you have to deny the children of Parks the reading of books which have been enjoyed by my children as well as so many others?" The board professed ignorance of the administration's actions and appeared unaware of a board policy that opposed book censorship. Unlike the fourth-grader who started the controversy, Morris's bad dream didn't end, and the banning remained in force.

Landmark Challenge: "Manageable Chills" in Minnesota

Some challengers read only selected passages or none of a book before bringing a challenge against it. But Margaret Byron was thorough. This parent of a child at Johnsville Elementary School in Anoka, Minnesota, read three of the nine *Goosebumps* books in the school library before bringing her complaint before the Anoka-Hennepin District 11 school system in the spring of 1996.

"I would like to see the school remove the books from the media center," she wrote. "While the books are only fiction and unreal, children under the age of twelve, as well as many teenagers, may not be able to handle the frightening content of the books. Some children could become paranoid and insecure about daily life after reading the books. The book covers alone are quite offensive." The nine challenged titles included *The Haunted Mask, It Came from Beneath the Sink,* and *A Shocker on Shock Street.*

An eight-member school committee formed to review the materials and the challenge. It was composed of the school's principal, teachers, the librarian, parents, and several other citizens. The committee's vote on the challenge was split; a second committee considered an appeal from Byron. During this time, the nine *Goosebumps* books remained on the library shelves.

In January 1997, the committee held two hearings and heard from ninety speakers, including many children who defended the books. "If somebody can't handle the *Goosebumps* books, they shouldn't read them," said student Patrick Murphy. "But don't wreck it for me." A number of parents felt quite differently. Arguments that the books motivated reluctant readers to read did not impress parent Barbara Anderson. "I'm just amazed and appalled that the only way you people can get your children to read books is to let them read this type of garbage," she said. District residents mailed the committee more than 400 letters, most of them favoring the retention of the challenged books.

On February 3, after a six-hour meeting, the committee announced that it had unanimously decided that the *Goosebumps* books had educational benefits and should remain available to students. In its report, the committee stated that the books give readers "chills which are manageable; they allow a child to work out his or her own strategy for dealing with the possibility of real threat . . . Students have the right to choose their own reading materials. The responsibility for good decision-making regarding reading choices should rest between an individual child and the child's parents." The committee pointed out that the books encourage reluctant readers with basic vocabulary; simple, repetitive plots; and imaginative story lines.

"Kids that read them actually love them," said committee head and parent Wendy Graves. "They race to get them. They don't stay long on the shelf." Margaret Byron found the decision "a big letdown." "I wish," she said, "they had at least put parental restrictions on them."

Further Reading

Allen, Jamie. "Welcome to R. L. Stine's 'Nightmare.'" CNN.com, October 29, 1999. Available online: http://edition.cnn.com/books/news/9910/29/rl.stine. Accessed November 29, 2007.

"Anoka, Minnesota." *Newsletter on Intellectual Freedom*, March 1997: 36.

Becker, Beverly C., and Susan M. Stans. *Hit List for Children 2: Frequently Challenged Books*. Chicago: American Library Association, 2002.

Finn, Peter. "Horror Books the Rage of Young Readers; Genre's Grip on Children Gives Some Adults Goose Bumps." *Washington Post*, March 11, 1996: B.01.

Foerstel, Herbert N. *Banned in the U.S.A.: A Reference Guide to Book Censorship in School and Public Libraries*. Westport, Conn.: Greenwood Press, 2002.

"Minneapolis, Minnesota." *Newsletter on Intellectual Freedom*, May 1997: 77.

"Parks, Arizona." *Newsletter on Intellectual Freedom*, March 1997: 33.

Saillant, Catherine. "Getting Goosebumps; Popularity of Scary Stories Please Some, Perturbs Others." *Los Angeles Times*, October 30, 1995: 1.

Tabor, Mary B. W. "Hints of Horror, Shouts of Protest." *New York Times*, April 2, 1997: B.6. Available online: http://query.nytimes.com/gst/fullpage.html?res=9D0DE0DE163DF931A35757C0A96 1958260&sec=&spon=&partner=permalink&exprod=permalink. Accessed January 4, 2008.

About the Author of the *Goosebumps* Books

R. L. Stine (1943–   )

Horror and humor have been the hallmarks of R. L. Stine's work throughout his prolific career. Robert Lawrence Stine was born on October 8, 1943, in Columbus, Ohio. His father was a shipping clerk. Young Robert found an old typewriter in the attic and began to write jokes and stories. He later attended Ohio State University, where he was the editor of the campus humor magazine. After graduating in 1965, he moved to New York City to pursue a writing career. Stine found work at Scholastic, Inc., where he created and edited the humor magazine *Bananas* for ten years. He also wrote numerous joke books for Scholastic under the name "Jovial Bob Stine."

In 1989, Stine co-created Nickelodeon's television series *Eureeka's Castle* (1989–95) and he also served as head writer. Working with his wife, Jane, publisher of Parachute Press, he created and wrote his first young-adult horror series, *Fear Street* (1989–97) and then launched *Goosebumps* in 1992. It quickly became one of the best-selling children's book series of all time. In the early 2000s, Stine wrote installments of three new book series, *Mostly Ghostly*, *Rotten School*, and a revived *Fear Street*. He has also written an autobiography, *It Came From Ohio!: My Life as a Writer* (1998), and an adult horror novel, *Superstitious* (1996).

In 2003, the *Guinness Book of World Records* named Stine the best-selling children's book series author of all time. With *Goosebumps* and his other series, Stine has more than fulfilled his goal of writing "scary books that are also funny."

The Giver (1993)
by Lois Lowry

What Happens in *The Giver*

The futuristic world that twelve-year-old Jonas and his family live in seems perfect. It has no crime, illness, or poverty. Everyone has meaningful work and appears happy and content but are devoid of strong feelings of hate or love. Jonas's mother is a government lawyer and his father a nurturer, a person who cares for newborn children before other families adopt them. One of these children is Gabriel, an infant that Jonas and his sister, Lily, become attached to.

At the Ceremony of Twelve, a rite of passage for children, Jonas and his schoolmates are given their career assignments. Jonas receives the great honor of becoming a Receiver of Memory. He spends his days with an old man, called the Giver, who transfers by touch the collective memories of their civilization to Jonas. Some of these memories are pleasant ones, such as memories of Christmases past, while others are painful and troubling—the chaos and death of war and the slaughtering of animals. The Receiver of Memory keeps these memories and does not share them with the rest of the people who could be harmed by them.

One day, when he has received all the memories from the Giver, Jonas will replace him. But Jonas accidentally learns the horrible truth about his orderly world, and everything changes. The Giver shows him a video of his own father "releasing" a child born a twin. Jonas thought to be "released" meant to be sent away to another place, but he watches in horror as his loving father injects the baby with a deadly drug and then calmly disposes of the body. The old, the sickly, and unwanted newborns are all put to death this way.

Jonas decides to flee, with the Giver's blessing, to "Elsewhere," a fabled alternate land where feelings and love are kept alive. Jonas, learning that Gabriel is to be released, takes the child with him into the forest. After days of deprivation, they are close to death. Then, Jonas reaches his goal, a sled atop a mountain. With Gabriel beside him, he rides down the mountain. "Downward, downward, faster and faster," Lowry writes in the book's final moments. "Suddenly he [Jonas] was aware with certainty and joy that below, ahead, they were waiting for him; and that they were waiting, too, for the baby. For the first time, he heard something that he knew to be music. He heard people singing."

Challenges and Censorship

The Giver is in a grand tradition of dystopian literature that includes such classic novels as Aldous Huxley's *Brave New World* and George Orwell's *1984*. As opposed to utopian literature, which depicts future societies that are ideal, this genre displays a dark future where humankind has not learned from its mistakes but has raised them to a new level of infamy. Hailed as a remarkable book on its publication in 1993, *The Giver* was awarded the Newbery Medal in 1994. "*The Giver* is a warning in narrative form," wrote children's author Natalie Babbitt in her review of the novel. "It is beautiful." "The story is skillfully written; the air of disquiet is delicately insinuated," wrote a reviewer in *Horn Book*. "And the theme of balancing the values of freedom and security is beautifully presented."

Yet the novel has stirred great controversy in schools and libraries. It is ranked fourteenth on the American Library Association's "100 Most Frequently Challenged Books of 1990–2000." "I think it's an honor I would prefer to forgo," author Lois Lowry once said. "It's a difficult situation." As Lowry is quick to point out, the book contains neither bad language nor explicit sex. But it raises other disturbing issues—including infanticide, euthanasia, and other forms of violence against people and animals—that have led many parents and school officials to challenge it.

According to Lowry, "the whole concept of memory is one that interests me a great deal. I'm not sure why that is, but I've always been fascinated by the thought of what memory is and what it does and how it works and what we learn from it. And so I think probably that interest of my own and that particular subject was the origin, one of many, of *The Giver*."

The Giver is the first volume in a loose trilogy that includes *Gathering Blue* (2000) and *Messenger* (2004). Although the settings and characters are different in each book, they are linked by similar themes that include, according to the author, "the vital need of people to be aware of their interdependence not only with each other, but with the world and its environment."

Landmark Challenge: Defending Books That Expose "The Dark Side" of Life

When a group of parents led by Eileen Casper challenged *The Giver* as suggested reading for eighth-graders in Blue Springs, Missouri, middle schools in the fall of 2003, it was just the beginning of a widespread movement for censorship.

Calling the novel "lewd" and "twisted," the group of parents asked that *The Giver* be removed from all district schools. A communication arts committee heard the challenge and voted to keep the book. The parents appealed to a second committee, sending it their written objections. That committee, too, supported keeping the book. Because the challengers were not allowed to attend the meeting, they insisted the district had violated its own law on open meetings and sought the advice of an attorney. The district replied through its attorney that it did not deliberately exclude them from the meeting.

The Blue Springs school board announced in December 2003 that its members would read *The Giver* and come to a decision about the book within several months. But while the board deliberated, Casper and other parents were at work examining all books in the school curriculum to decide whether they were appropriate. "Books—from elementary up—that if they were made into movies would be rated R," Casper said. "Just by having several children in the schools we see what they are reading. They [school officials] call this curriculum critical thinking. It has a repetitive theme of violence and killing, euthanasia and sex." She added that her group was looking into a Web site, developed by other parents in the district, that listed books they found inappropriate for schoolchildren.

The school board's March 2005 meeting was packed with people eager to learn its decision. One after another, board members vowed that they would protect the right to read good books, such as *The Giver*, that depicted, in the words of one reporter from the *Kansas City Star*, "the dark side" of life. "We don't haphazardly create our curriculum," said the district's director of information services, "and we don't haphazardly change it."

"While districts all around the metropolitan area were busy removing challenged books from their curricula," wrote an observer from the National Council of Teachers of English (NCTE), "the Blue Springs Board of Education stood firm." For doing so, the board was the recipient of the NCTE SLATE (Support for the Learning and Teaching of English) National Intellectual Freedom Award in 2006.

Further Reading

Babbitt, Natalie. "The Hidden Cost of Contentment." *Washington Post*, May 9, 1993: X.15.

Becker, Beverly C., and Susan M. Stans. *Hit List for Children 2: Frequently Challenged Books*. Chicago: American Library Association, 2002.

"Blue Springs, Missouri." *Newsletter on Intellectual Freedom*, March 2005: 57–58. Available online: https://members.ala.org/nif/v54n2/dateline.html. Accessed December 14, 2007.

Foerstel, Herbert N. *Banned in the U.S.A.: A Reference Guide to Book Censorship in Schools and Public Libraries*. Westport, Conn.: Greenwood Press, 2002.

Hatcher, Thurston. "Book Challenges Drop, But Librarians, Writers Remain Wary." CNN.com, September 26, 2000. Available online: http://archives.cnn.com/2000/books/news/09/26/banned.books/index.html. Accessed November 27, 2007.

Lois Lowry official website. Available online: www.loislowry.com. Accessed November 27, 2007.

National Council of Teachers of English Web site. "NCTE SLATE Gives Three National Intellectual Freedom Awards." Available online: www.ncte.org/about/issues/censorship/awards/125602.htm. Accessed November 27, 2007.

Zammarelli, Chris. "God Is Not Pleased With You." Bookslut.com, March 2004. Available online: www.bookslut.com/banned_bookslut/2004_03_001684.php. Accessed December 14, 2007.

About the Author of *The Giver*

Lois Lowry (1937–   )

Lois Lowry has written a wide range of fiction for young adults, from lighthearted contemporary comedy to dark futuristic fables. She was born Lois Ann Hammersburg on March 20, 1937, in Hawaii, where her father, an Army dentist, was stationed at the time. As a child, she moved frequently with her family from one Army post to another, including two years spent in Japan.

She attended Brown University in Providence, Rhode Island, from 1954 to 1956, but left school after marrying Donald Lowry, a Navy officer. They had four children together. Like Lois's father, Donald's duties took the family from one post to another. They finally settled in Maine, where Lois returned to college and completed a degree in English literature at the University of Southern Maine in Portland in 1972.

Lowry found work as a freelance journalist and photographer. Her first novel, *A Summer to Die* (1977), was based on the death of her older sister, Helen, at age twenty-eight. Lowry divorced her husband that same year. More books followed, including *Autumn Street* (1980), her most autobiographical novel, and *Anastasia Krupnik* (1979), the first of nine popular novels about a precocious ten-year-old girl. In 1988, Lowry began a second series of books about Anastasia's brother, Sam. She was awarded the Newbery Medal twice, in 1990 for *Number the Stars* (1989) and in 1994 for *The Giver* (1993).

Lowry's son Grey, a fighter pilot, died in a plane crash in 1995. She lives with her long-time companion, Martin Small, in Massachusetts and Maine.

"My books have varied in content and style," she has written on her website. "Yet it seems that all of them deal, essentially, with the same general theme: the importance of human connections."

His Dark Materials Trilogy
(1995–2000)
by Philip Pullman

What Happens in the *His Dark Materials* Trilogy

In the first volume of this fantasy trilogy, *Northern Lights* (published as *The Golden Compass* in the United States), the young heroine, Lyra Belacqua, travels to the remote north to find and rescue her best friend and other children. They are being held there by the Magisterium, an all-controlling global authority connected with the Roman Catholic Church. The captive children are being used in experiments with Dust, strange particles that are associated with the Christian concept of original sin. Together with her soul companion, Pantalaiman, a shape-shifting creature known as a daemon, Lyra and her father set off to find the source of Dust.

In *The Subtle Knife*, Lyra reaches the techno-city of Cittàgazze, controlled by the dangerous Specters. Here she meets Will Parry, a twelve-year-old boy from her own world. Will possesses the Subtle Knife, a magical weapon capable of cutting portals into other worlds. Will goes to find Lyra's father to give him the knife to fight the Authority, the head of the Magisterium. Meanwhile, Lyra is kidnapped by her own mother, Mrs. Coulter, who works for the Magisterium.

In the final volume, *The Amber Spyglass*, Will rescues Lyra and together they travel to the Land of the Dead to free ghosts trapped there by the Authority. The bold scientist Mary Malone uncovers the truth about Dust: it is not sinful, but an agent of self-awareness. Mrs. Coulter is reconciled with her husband and together they destroy the Authority's Regent Metatron, and die themselves in the struggle. A final climactic battle ensues between the Authority's army and the rebels. Evil is defeated and the Authority dies. Will and Lyra find true love, but in order to prevent the flow of Dust, they must remain apart, closing the portals to their two separate worlds.

Challenges and Censorship

While the *Harry Potter* books have stirred many Christian groups with their focus on the occult and witchcraft, this other fantasy series from England has been condemned even more harshly for its alleged attack on organized religion, specifically the Roman Catholic Church. The question of whether the author, Philip Pullman, a professed atheist, is promoting atheism or simply attacking the distortion of Christianity by earthly leaders is debatable. School challenges to the books have been few to date, simply because the books are not as well known in this country as the *Harry Potter* series. Those challenges that have occurred in the U.S. have largely been based on the trilogy's anti-church stance.

Author Philip Pullman claims to have written his trilogy, whose title comes from poet John Milton's epic *Paradise Lost*, in response to Christian writer C. S. Lewis's fantasy series *The Chronicles of Narnia*. "I hate them [the Lewis books] with a deep and bitter passion," Pullman once said, "with their view of childhood as a golden age from which sexuality and adulthood are a falling away."

The story of his trilogy developed slowly for Pullman. "I knew I wanted it to deal with basic, enormous issues, such as the difference between innocence and awareness, freedom and tyranny, good and evil, ignorance and wisdom. These ideas have their basis in the Bible, in the story of Adam and Eve, and have been told by many authors before me." He is also quick to say that his books take issue not with religion per se, but with those who "misuse religion, or any other kind of doctrine with a holy book" in order "to dominate and suppress human freedoms."

Landmark Challenge:
Don't Read the Book, Don't Watch the Movie

New Line Cinema thought that by removing the anti-religious elements from its film adaptation of *The Golden Compass*, it would avoid controversy. But it was wrong. A number of religious groups saw the movie as more dangerous. They felt that by watering down the author's message it would encourage young people to read "atheistic" literature.

"These books denigrate Christianity, trash the Catholic Church, and sell the virtues of atheism," claimed William A. Donohue, president of the Catholic League for Religious and Civil Rights. Two months before the movie's release in the United States in December 2007, he called on Christians to boycott it.

In the trilogy, the central force of evil is a governing body called "The Church," that reports directly to the "Vatican Council." In the film, most references to the Catholic Church have been removed, although the name "the Magisterium," referring to the Roman Catholic Church's official teaching authority, has been retained. The film's theme of organized religion being a dangerous and suppressive force in society has been largely removed, and *The Golden Compass* has been marketed as a children's fantasy film.

"The religion was never a reason to make the movie, or not to make it," said Toby Emmerich, president of New Line Cinema the film's producer. "I always felt the heart of the story was the relationship between Lyra and Iorek [a polar bear she befriends] . . . It's a story about a little girl creating a new family for herself."

Donahue admitted the movie was "fairly innocuous" but claimed it was "bait for the books: unsuspecting parents who take their children to see the movie may feel impelled to buy the three books as a Christmas present." For this reason, he accused the movie makers of participating in a "deceitful, stealth campaign."

But not all Christian organizations saw Pullman's message as an atheistic one. "It undoubtedly makes people question, but inspires them to look harder for more authentic religion," claimed Brian Detweiler, co-director of Reel Spirituality, a think tank at Fuller Theological Seminary in Pasadena, California. "Pullman takes license in pointing out the scary, false gods and destructive idols we've created. In that sense, I think he's doing a great service."

The U.S. Conference of Catholic Bishops also believed the books were in line with Catholic theology. "To the extent, moreover, that Lyra and her allies are taking a stand on behalf of free will in opposition to the coercive force of the Magisterium, they are of course acting entirely in harmony with Catholic teaching," they stated in their review of the movie. "The heroism and self-sacrifice that they demonstrate provide appropriate moral lessons for viewers."

Donna Freitas, a Catholic theologian, went even further in her praise of the work. "His [Pullman's] trilogy is not filled with attacks on Christianity, but with attacks on authorities who claim access to one true interpretation of a religion. Pullman's work is filled with the feminist and liberation strands of Catholic theology that have sustained my own faith, and which threaten the power structure of the church. Pullman's work is not anti-Christian, but anti-orthodox."

But for those who were anti-religious, the film was a grave disappointment. "It was clear right from the start that the makers of this film intended to take out the anti-religious elements of Pullman's book," said Terry Sanderson, president of the National Secular Society of Britain. "In doing that they are taking the heart out of it, losing the point of it, castrating it. It seems that religion has now completely conquered America's cultural life and it is much the poorer for it. What a shame that we have to endure such censorship here too." Although Pullman himself is an honorary associate of the National Secular Society and a professed secularist, he said in an interview that he was "very happy" with the movie version.

Chris Weitz, the film's screenwriter and director, is not content to leave out the religious element in the remaining films of the trilogy if they are made. "I mean to protect the integrity of those remaining chapters," he said. "The aim is to put in the elements we need to make this movie a hit so that we can be much less compromising in how the second and third books are shot."

This cannot be good news for the Catholic League. According to president Donahue's Web site, "The second book of the trilogy, 'The Subtle Knife,' is more overt in its hatred of Christianity than the first book, and the third entry, 'The Amber Spyglass,' is even more blatant."

Whether these movies are made is still undecided: *The Golden Compass* was only a modest box-office success in the United States, but it did much better business abroad.

Further Reading

Freitas, Donna. "God in the Dust: What Catholics Attacking 'The Golden Compass' Are Really Afraid Of." *Boston Globe*, November 25, 2007: D.1. Available online: www.boston.com/bostonglobe/ideas/articles/2007/11/25/god_in_the_dust. Accessed December 14, 2007.

Loer, Stephanie. "Author's Trilogy Inspired by Milton's 'Paradise Lost': Philip Pullman Tackles Life's Powerful Themes." *Boston Globe*, December 3, 2000: L.14.

McGrath, Charles. "Unholy Production with a Fairy-Tale Ending." *New York Times*, December 2, 2007: A&L.1, 16. Available online: www.nytimes.com/2007/12/02/movies/02mcgr.html. Accessed December 15, 2007.

Phan, Katherine T. "Christian Groups Claim Religion-Purged 'Golden Compass' Movie Promotes Pro-Atheism Books." Christian Post Online, October 31, 2007. Available online: www.christianpost.com/article/20071031/29901_Christian_Groups_Claim_Religion-Purged_'Golden_Compass'_Movie_Promotes_Pro-Atheism_Books.htm. Accessed December 14, 2007.

Weiss, Jeffrey. "A Stirring Flick: 'Golden Compass' Brings Religious Controversy." *Connecticut Post*, December 15, 2007: B1.

About the Author of *His Dark Materials*

Philip Pullman (1946–   )

Philip Pullman was born on October 19, 1946, in Norwich, Norfolk County, Great Britain. His father was a pilot for the Royal Air Force (RAF) and the family traveled from military outpost to outpost when Pullman was a child. He lived for a time in Rhodesia (now the independent nation of Zimbabwe), Africa. His father died in a plane crash when Pullman was seven. His mother remarried, and the family moved to Australia.

Pullman attended Exeter College at Oxford University in England and graduated in 1968. He became a teacher and married Judith Speller in 1970. He published his first novel, *The Haunted Storm*, in 1972. This was followed by an adult fantasy novel, *Galatea* (1978), and his first children's book, *Count Karlstein* (1982). From 1988 to 1996, Pullman taught part time at Westminster College in Oxford.

He began his most celebrated work to date, the *His Dark Materials* trilogy, in 1993. The first volume, *Northern Lights*, appeared in 1995. It was awarded the Carnegie Medal, a British children's fiction award. The second volume, *The Subtle Knife*, was published in 1997 and the third, *The Amber Spyglass*, in 2000. All three books were published in one collected volume in 2007.

In 2008, Pullman was working on a sequel to the trilogy, *The Book of Dust*. He was a joint winner of the Astrid Lindgren Memorial Award for children's literature in 2005 and is a supporter of the British Humanist Association.

The *Harry Potter* Books (1997–2007)
by J. K. Rowling

What Happens in the *Harry Potter* Books

Harry Potter is the hero of a series of seven novels that chart his adventures as a wizard in training at the Hogwarts School of Witchcraft and Wizardry in England. At the start of *Harry Potter and the Sorcerer's Stone* (published in the United Kingdom as *Harry Potter and the Philosopher's Stone*; 1997), Harry is an orphan. His parents, both wizards, had been killed earlier by the evil wizard Lord Voldemort. Harry lives with his aunt and uncle, the Dursleys, who mistreat him, favoring their own son, Harry's selfish cousin. Despite the Dursleys' efforts to thwart any inclination Harry has inherited toward magic, he is invited to matriculate at Hogwarts and begin his education in wizardry.

At Hogwarts, Harry develops his skills in magic under the benevolent headmaster Albus Dumbledore; becomes best friends with fellow students Ron Weasley and Hermione Granger; makes an enemy out of another student, Draco Malfoy; and learns to excel at the flying broomstick game of Quidditch. In the course of the book, one of the teachers is exposed as the agent of Voldemort and dies in pursuit of the Sorcerer's Stone, which grants its owner eternal life. Each subsequent book in the series takes place during a year in Harry's life at Hogwarts.

In *Harry Potter and the Chamber of Secrets* (1998), Harry must hunt down a monstrous snake, the Basilisk, that is turning Hogwarts students to stone. Voldemort uses Ron's younger sister, Ginny, as his agent, but Harry saves her and breaks the force of evil that possesses her.

In *Harry Potter and the Prisoner of Azkaban* (1999), the title character, Sirius Black, reveals himself to be Harry's uncle. Black supposedly was imprisoned for betraying Harry's parents to Voldemort, but the charge proves to be untrue.

In *Harry Potter and the Goblet of Fire* (2000), Voldemort returns and faces Harry in a one-on-one duel at the climax of the Triwizard Tournament at Hogwarts. The fight ends in a draw, but Harry emerges from it with new strength and maturity.

Dumbledore is replaced as headmaster by Professor Umbridge, who represents the Ministry of Magic in *Harry Potter and the Order of the Phoenix* (2003). Sirius Black is killed by his own sister, an agent of Voldemort, and Harry discovers that the father of his nemesis at school, Draco, is also one of Voldemort's minions. The book ends with Dumbledore being reinstated as headmaster.

In *Harry Potter and the Half-Blood Prince* (2005), Dumbledore is killed by the teacher, Professor Snape, who is revealed as the half-blood prince and goes to see Voldemort. Harry begins a new romance with Ginny Weasley.

In the final book, *Harry Potter and the Deathly Hallows* (2007), Hogwarts is no longer safe for Harry. The Ministry of Magic has fallen, and Voldemort's power increases. But in the end, Harry triumphs over evil, and Hermione and Ron's relationship finally blossoms into romance.

Challenges and Censorship

The seven novels that make up the *Harry Potter* series are among the best-selling children's books in history. They are also one of the most challenged group of books in modern times. The reason for the countless challenges and bannings can be summed up in one terse quote from a Michigan challenge of 2000: "The books are based on sorcery, which is an abomination to the Lord."

Not long after the first book, *Harry Potter and the Sorcerer's Stone*, was published in the United States by Scholastic in 1998, fundamentalist Christian groups began to voice their disapproval. The book focuses on "a serious tone of death, hate, lack of respect, and sheer evil," declared a challenge that year in South Carolina. A 2000 challenge in Alabama made the connection to religion versus occult even clearer. "It was a mistake years ago to take prayer out of the schools because it let Satanism in," said the challenge. "We need to put God back in [our] schools and throw *Harry Potter* books out."

Other challenges have found the behavior of Harry and his fellow wizard students reprehensible from a less religious, more ethical base. "[The books are] telling children over and over again that lying, cheating, and stealing are not only acceptable, but that they're cool and cute," claimed a Pennsylvania challenge in 2002.

And it hasn't only been conservative Christians and more secular ethicists who have gotten on Harry's case. The books were banned in the United Arab Emirates in 2001 because they espoused "written or illustrated material that contradicts Islamic and Arab values."

But Harry's supporters have, in many cases, been just as determined in defending the series. Dismissing the elements of sorcery and magic as just good fun, they praise Rowling's ability to make avid readers out of previously reluctant ones. "It has brought a new generation to reading, got kids absorbed in huge hefty hardbacks the way they wouldn't have been," said Joel Rickett, news editor of *The Bookseller*. While questions remain about whether this reading mania will carry over to other good literature now that the cycle is finished, other readers are impressed by some of the same issues that bothered the books' critics—death, loss, and a dark tone.

Rowling herself experienced the death of her mother from multiple sclerosis shortly after she began writing the books, and she claims it helped her decide on the series' central theme—a young man dealing with loss. "I think children are very scared of this stuff even if they haven't experienced it," said the author about the death of a loved one. "And I think the way to meet that is head-on. I absolutely believe, as a writer and as a parent, that the solution is not to pretend things don't happen but to examine them, in a loving, safe way."

There has been little that is "loving" about the attacks against the books, which have included a disturbing number of book burnings across the nation. Although the *Harry Potter* books did not begin appearing in the United States until 1997, the first three managed to score enough challenges to rank seventh on the American Library Association's "100 Most Frequently Challenged Books of 1990–2000." From 1999 to 2002, a *Harry Potter* title topped the ALA's annual "10 Most Frequently Challenged Books" list, ranking second in 2003.

Landmark Challenge:
Banning without Banning in Michigan

On November 22, 1999, school superintendent Gary Feenstra of Zeeland, Michigan, sent a memo to all teachers. After receiving complaints from parents at three elementary schools, Feenstra was instructing teachers not to read any *Harry Potter* books aloud in their classrooms. He further ordered that the books be restricted in school libraries to only those students who had written permission from a parent to take them out.

Many teachers and students were incensed by the memo. "By placing restrictions, he took the decision out of the hands of the people it belongs in—the parents and the kids," said Jim Dana, executive director of the Great Lakes Booksellers Association and husband of Mary Dana, a middle school teacher and leader in the protest. She sent the school board a letter opposing the memo that was co-signed by forty other teachers.

But the board staunchly supported the superintendent's actions. "I have the utmost confidence in Feenstra," said board president Tom Bock. "The decision he's made is a good one." "We have never said the kids can't read the book," reasoned communication coordinator Jim Camenga. "We're trying to say that parents have a right to have input on what their child reads."

Few opposers were convinced by this argument. "He's [Feenstra's] banned it without banning it," said third-grade teacher Mary Shannon, another leader in the protest. "He skirted around the issue. It's so frustrating. They're not improving the relationship between the board, the superintendent, and the teachers."

Soon outside organizations were joining the fight, in defense of the books. They included the Association of American Publishers (AAP), the National Council of Teachers of English (NCTE), and Scholastic, Inc., the books' American publisher.

A school board meeting held on February 21, 2000, was well attended. Some twenty-three people spoke, about equally split for and against Feenstra's stance. "I'm here tonight to ask the board to free Harry Potter," said Mary VanHarn. "I could teach Sunday school with these books." Parent Mary Elzings acknowledged the books' virtues, but still supported the superintendent's decision. "There is no doubt this is a phenomenal author," she said. "It's whether or not our children are ready to handle this." The board took no action that evening.

When the board met again on March 20, Feenstra appeared to be willing to compromise. Although he said at the meeting that he was not rescinding his memo, he agreed that opposing parents' concerns needed to be addressed. He agreed to the formation of a fourteen-member committee to reconsider the *Harry Potter* books and reach a recommendation for the school board by May 1. At that time, the superintendent said he would "seriously consider and accept, change, or reject" the committee's recommendation. Parent reaction was mixed. "It's what I wanted," said Mary Ockerse. "We wished this would have happened in the beginning."

But the committee, once formed, worked in secret. The public was not invited to attend its meetings nor were the members even identified. Just when it looked like the controversy would drag on, the committee announced its recommendation. It was in favor of removing all but one restriction from the *Harry Potter* books. Its decision met with Feenstra's full approval. The one restriction that remained was that teachers from kindergarten through fifth grade would not be allowed to read aloud to their classes from Rowling's books.

That September, as a new school year was starting, Mary Dana and parent Nancy Zennie were honored by the AAP at the Library of Congress for their efforts to end the restrictions on the *Harry Potter* books. The AAP recognized them as individuals who "put their belief in the principle of freedom to read into action." Surprised but happy to be so honored, Dana said, "The whole issue of freedom to read is integral. Children have rights, too."

Jim Camenga, speaking for the administration of the Zeeland Public Schools, was muted in his praise for the two women. "We respect their right to celebrate their efforts," he said. He also announced that the fourth Rowling novel, *Harry Potter and the Goblet of Fire*, would soon be in all district elementary and middle school libraries.

Landmark Challenge:
A Parent Speaks Up for Harry

Parents are usually the instigators of book challenges in schools, but not Larry Finch, father of a fifth-grader at Bullard Talent Elementary School in Fresno, California. Finch, an electrician, stepped in to rescue *Harry Potter* and uncovered a rather complicated cover-up. It began in late 2000, when Finch's daughter came home to tell him that her teacher said she couldn't read *Harry Potter* books in the class's daily read-aloud time. When he asked district officials why Rowling's books weren't being read, he was told a religious group had expressed concern about the series, claiming it advocated witchcraft and the occult among students. This led the officials to issue a mandate banning the use of the book in the classroom.

"This is censorship," insisted Finch, "and censorship is wrong." Carol Bloesser, the district's deputy superintendent for standards and accountability, didn't see it that way. "There is no ban on poor Harry," she said. "We just asked teachers to be cautious. If you're using *Harry Potter*, think about its instructional value and be cautious that some parents may not want their kids to read it."

Finch disputed Bloesser's statement, claiming that she and the school's principal had told him earlier that teachers could not read aloud from the *Harry Potter* books. "'Now, Dr. Bloesser says, 'No, you didn't [hear that]. We were only cautioning them,'" Finch said. "If we're going to step into the area of censorship, let's put it on the front burner and in a spot where we all can discuss it."

Landmark Challenge:
Burning a "Masterpiece of Satanic Deception"

"Behind that innocent face is the power of satanic darkness," said Jack Brock, pastor of the Christ Community Church in Alamogordo, New Mexico. "Harry Potter is the devil and he is destroying people."

Rather than allow the destruction to continue, Pastor Brock decided to destroy Harry Potter, or at least the books his adventures are described in. On December 30, 2001, Brock conducted one of the more publicized book burnings in the United States in recent years. Hundreds of congregants from Brock's church gathered outside the church building after a prayer service that lasted about half an hour.

As the event began, about 800 counterprotestors stood and watched disapprovingly from across the street. Some carried signs of protests. One read: "Hitler—Bin Laden—Pastor Brock—What great company." Others wore black witch hats and carried brooms. "Burning books leads to ignorance and that's why I'm standing out here," said Vicky O'Reilly, whose son is an avid fan of *Harry Potter*.

Before the actual book burning commenced, Brock gave a sermon, declaring that fire was cleansing and that the event was just a part of a major Christian movement for the faithful to divest themselves of all items that cut them off from communication with God. These included not only the *Harry Potter* books, which he had called "a masterpiece of Satanic deception," but also the *Lord of the Rings* series by J. R. R. Tolkien, horror novels by Stephen King, and, oddly enough, a copy of *The Complete Works of William Shakespeare*. Magazines like *Cosmopolitan* and *YM* were also tossed into the bonfire, along with such "satanic" music as AC/DC and Eminem CDs. Ouija boards, supposedly a way to communicate with the spirit world, were consigned to the flames as well.

Some residents did more than protest the book burning. The Alamogordo Public Library defiantly extended a *Harry Potter* display that was timed to coincide with the movie debut of *Harry Potter and the Sorcerer's Stone*, the first film adaptation of the series. Those residents who saw the books as a positive reading experience for children gave money to the library to buy more books. "With this money we are purchasing additional copies of *Harry Potter*, Tolkien, and Shakespeare," said library director Jim Preston. Pastor Brock himself admitted to never having read any of Harry's adventures, but claimed to have "researched" the books' contents.

While Brock's book burning may not have achieved its goal, the pastor can take heart that his event was more successful than a similar one held in Lewiston, Maine, only a few weeks earlier. The Jesus Party, a local church group, was denied a permit by the Lewiston Fire Department to burn the *Harry Potter* books. Led by the Rev. Douglas Turner, the group decided to turn their book burning into a "book cutting." Supplied with scissors, Turner and his followers cut up copies of all four of the *Harry Potter* books published to that date. "It's no secret that I enjoy what I'm doing right now," Turner declared as he cut through a copy of one of Rowling's novels.

Landmark Challenge:
Harry Potter and the Persistent Parent

Laura Mallory is a former Christian missionary, and she brought a missionary's zeal to her campaign to ban every *Harry Potter* book from the largest school district in the state of Georgia. The Loganville parent of three made her first complaint against *Harry Potter and the Sorcerer's Stone* to the Gwinnett County school district in September 2005. The complaint was considered by a media review panel at her children's school, J. C. Magill Elementary School in Suwanee, and rejected. "I support the value of the *Harry Potter* books to develop children's imagination and ability to read," said school board member Mary Kay Murphy.

Under further pressure from Mallory and her supporters, the board held a public hearing on April 20, 2006. "I want to protect children from evil, not fill their minds with it," Mallory declared. "The *Harry Potter* books teach children and adults that witchcraft is OK for children." Supporters of the books countered that the most positive theme to emerge from the series was the triumph of good over evil and that no books had been as successful in turning children on to the joys of reading.

On May 11, the county school board voted on Mallory's challenge and unanimously rejected it. "At the very heart of this issue is censorship," said board member Carole Boyce shortly before the vote. "Our students do understand the difference between fact and fiction."

"I knew what they were going to do," said Mallory after the decision, "but it's good we live in a country where you can stand up for what you believe in. God is alive and real and he says it [witchcraft] is an abomination. How can we say it is good reading material?"

Blog postings had drawn the world's attention to Gwinnett County and the controversy. To remove the books, insisted hearing officer SuEllen Bray, "would open this very fine school system to ridicule by many of its citizens as well as citizens of the nation."

But Mallory persisted and took her anti-Rowling campaign to the state level. On December 14, 2006, the state board of education decided to let the books remain in the schools. Undaunted, on January 9, 2007, Mallory filed an appeal in the county's superior court after receiving what she called a "very specific answer to prayer." The appeal was again turned down.

While this latest blow discouraged Mallory, it might not have stung so much as another development. In July 2007, her hometown of Loganville was named as one of thirteen "most *Harry Potter* towns" in Georgia, according to a survey conducted by Amazon.com, the mammoth book-selling Web site.

Further Reading

"Fresno, California," *Newsletter on Intellectual Freedom*, January 2001: 12.

"Harry Potter Books Burn as Library Showcases Rowling Titles." *American Libraries*, January 7, 2002. Available online: www.ala.org/ala/alonline/currentnews/newsarchive/2002/january2002/harrypotterbooks.cfm#potterburn. Accessed December 7, 2007.

"Harry Potter's Georgia Adventure to Continue." *American Libraries*, January 19, 2007. Available online: www.ala.org/ala/alonline/currentnews/newsarchive/2007/january2007/malloryappeal.cfm. Accessed December 7, 2007.

Kanavel, Nedra. "Book Ban Criticism Broadens to Nation." *Holland Sentinel*, February 4, 2000.

"Lewiston, Maine." *Newsletter on Intellectual Freedom*, January 2002: 24.

"'Satanic' Harry Potter Books Burnt." BBC News website, December 31, 2001. Available online: http://news.bbc.co.uk/2/hi/entertainment/1735623.stm. Accessed December 7, 2007.

"Suwanee, Georgia." *Newsletter on Intellectual Freedom*, July 2006: 207–208. Available online: https://members.ala.org/nif/v55n4/success_stories.html. Accessed December 7, 2007.

Whitcomb, Hillary. "Women Honored for Fight to Keep Potter on Shelves." *Holland Sentinel*, September 24, 2000.

Zammarelli, Chris. "A Masterpiece of Satanic Deception." Bookslut.com, July 2005. Available online: www.bookslut.com/banned_bookslut/2005_07_005957.php. Accessed December 7, 2007.

About the Author of the *Harry Potter* Books

J. K. Rowling (1965–   )

One of the best-selling children's authors of all time, J. K. Rowling's story is one of the most remarkable success stories in publishing history. She was born Joanne Kathleen Rowling on July 31, 1965, near the city of Bristol, England. She wrote her first story when she was five or six years old. She later attended the University of Exeter, majoring in French, with hopes of becoming a bilingual secretary. After graduation, Rowling pursued a secretarial career but found writing more interesting. At age twenty-six, she moved to Portugal to teach English. There she met and married journalist Jorge Arantes. The couple had a daughter, Jessica, in 1993. They divorced soon after and Rowling moved with Jessica to Edinburgh, Scotland, to be near her sister, Di, two years her junior.

Life was a struggle for the single mother, who lived for a time on welfare. While on a train from Manchester to London, she first got the idea for Harry Potter, taking the last name of childhood friends. She wrote much of the first book in restaurants where it was warm, saving on the heating bill in her tiny apartment. When she finished *Harry Potter and the Philosopher's Stone*, the novel was rejected numerous times before being bought by the publisher Bloomsbury for about $4,000. The book appeared in 1997 with a first printing of only 1,000 copies. It soon became a best seller in England as well as two years later in the United States, where the title was changed to *Harry Potter and the Sorcerer's Stone*.

Three more *Harry Potter* novels followed in quick succession, each selling more than the last. In the summer of 2000, the first three Potter books were numbers one, two, and three on the *New York Times* best-seller list. There were then more than 35 million copies of the four *Harry Potter* novels in print in thirty-five languages, including Latin and ancient Greek. That year, Rowling took a break from writing and met and later married Scottish doctor Neil Murray. *Harry Potter and the Order of the Phoenix* appeared in 2003, and *Harry Potter and the Half-Blood Prince* came out in 2005. The seventh and last book in the series, *Harry Potter and the Deathly Hallows*, appeared in 2007. After seventeen years of living with Harry and his friends (and enemies), Rowling says she is both "euphoric" and "devastated" to have finished the series, although she has not ruled out more *Harry Potter* books in the future.

Rowling currently lives in Edinburgh with her husband and their children, David and Mackenzie, and her daughter, Jessica, from her first marriage.

"I can never write anything as popular again," she says of the phenomenon of *Harry Potter*. ". . . I'll do exactly what I did with Harry—I'll write what I really want to write, and if it's something similar, that's OK, and if it's something very different, that's OK."

Blood and Chocolate (1997)
by Annette Curtis Klause

What Happens in *Blood and Chocolate*

Sixteen-year-old Vivian Gandillon is a werewolf who can change into a wolf at will. She lives in the suburbs of Maryland with her "pack." When a young boy werewolf kills a human girl, it leads to trouble. Vivian's father kills the guilty werewolf for endangering the pack, but vigilantes seek revenge and burn the house where the pack lives. Vivian's father and several others are killed, and the surviving pack members move to a new community.

Vivian enters a new high school and falls in love with Aiden, a human. Vivian's mother, Esmé, disapproves of her involvement with a human, and Gabriel, a young werewolf who becomes the new pack leader, pursues Vivian romantically, hoping to make her his "queen."

Vivian continues her relationship with Aiden and finally reveals her true nature to him. He is terrified and chases her away. Vivian soon believes she is the murderer of two humans, but then learns from her friends that she has been set up by the real killers, the jealous werewolf Astrid and another werewolf, Rafe. When Vivian visits Aiden again, he is prepared to shoot her with a silver bullet in order to kill her. But Astrid and Rafe show up, and Aiden, who now realizes that Vivian did not kill the humans, shoots Rafe dead.

Gabriel then arrives on the scene and kills Astrid. Terrified, Aiden fires at Gabriel, but Vivian steps into the line of fire and takes the bullet for him. Aiden flees and Vivian survives, but is stuck in "half-form," neither human nor wolf. When Gabriel shares his own personal tragedy with Vivian, they kiss and she is again able to transform into human and wolf form at will. Vivian finally realizes that she needs to stay with her own kind and accepts Gabriel as her mate.

Challenges and Censorship

The mixture of romance and horror in the fiction of Annette Curtis Klause has made *Blood and Chocolate* and her three other novels irresistible to young readers, especially girls. *Publishers Weekly* praised the novel on its publication in 1997 for its "darkly sexy prose and suspenseful storytelling." "Passion and philosophy dovetail superbly in this powerful, unforgettable novel for mature teens," wrote the reviewer for *Booklist*. *Kirkus Reviews* called the novel a "fierce, suspenseful chiller." *Blood and Chocolate* won the 1998 Young Adult Library Services Association (YALSA) Award for Best Book for Young Adults. The novel was loosely adapted into a film in 2007.

Some school officials and parents have found the novel too mature for teens, and in 2001 *Blood and Chocolate* ranked tenth on the American Library Association's "10 Most Frequently Challenged Books" for being "sexually explicit and unsuited to age group."

Referring to the difficulty of writing her books for young adults, Klause said, "The challenge is walking the fine line between the truth and what the publishers, parents, and the more conservative librarians want to hear . . . The challenge is to have characters that sound and act real without being accused of promoting promiscuity, bad language, and rampant drug use."

But Klause has also expressed her frustration with some of the challenges made against *Blood and Chocolate*. "I guess I get a little annoyed with people who read my books at a surface level," she has said. "There's no actual sex. It's steamy. That's all they see. I'm talking about the value of community and family. Yes, in this instance, this community happens to be a family of werewolves, but I'm using it as a metaphor for those tempestuous teenage years."

Landmark Challenge:
Changing Policy in La Porte

Sometimes a single book challenge can have far-reaching effects on censorship within a school system. This was certainly the case in La Porte, Texas, in 2001. Kimberly Lindquist, parent of a seventh-grader at Lomax Junior High School, brought a challenge against *Blood and Chocolate* before the La Porte Independent School District.

"It isn't the supernatural elements that bothered me so much," said Lindquist. "It is the twenty-three pages of sexual overtones. We all have adolescent longings, but that is not what we read in the pages of this book. There is no value in this book." Among the other objections to the novel Lindquist listed were profanity, drug and alcohol abuse, references to violence, and dark humor. She wanted the book removed from the libraries of both Lomax Junior High School and La Porte High School.

The board of trustees turned the matter over to an eleven-member review committee, which re-examined the book to see if it conformed to board book selection policy. In July, the committee made its recommendation to the trustees—to keep *Blood and Chocolate* in the two school libraries but remove it from any required reading lists.

The trustees met the following month but came to no decisive conclusion. They voted instead to temporarily pull the two existing copies of the book from the library shelves until they could review the book selection policy for how books are approved for the school curriculum. "As a policy-making body, we need to be cautious about making decisions on any individual item," said school superintendent John Sawyer. "You'll be asked more and more to do this . . . and that will bring you to your knees as a governing body. We need to look at the policy issue involved. We can define the mission a little bit plainer and hold this book in abeyance until we can adopt [a new or amended] policy."

Some trustees were skeptical about the way librarians chose books based on reviews in academic periodicals. "As part of the policy, we should ask people to actually read the book," said trustee Bill Baker, "and not just read reviews of the book." Others were worried that a negative response to *Blood and Chocolate* would lead to a rigidly conservative policy. "I would also be real careful so the policy doesn't become too restrictive," said trustee Chris Osten.

Kimberly Lindquist expressed satisfaction with the decision and hoped it would lead to a stricter policy. "This is going to do more ultimate good in screening out books," she said. "If they can change policy to make it easier to make decisions, that's a good idea."

Teachers at the two schools weren't so sure. They worried that once a book was called into question, there would be no stopping the filtering process. "It's very difficult," pointed out one administrator, "when junior high schools have students with maturity and reading levels that range from third to twelfth grade."

Author Annette Curtis Klause, who had been contacted about the controversy, agreed with this assessment. "It's based on cognitive levels, emotional levels, life experience, and the ability to put things into context," she said. "Seventh grade is sort of on the cusp for this book. Kids younger than that, I start to worry a little. You need to be of a certain maturity level to keep it in perspective. It's dealing with adolescents, and you shouldn't feel bad if you have these feelings. It's normal."

By December, the trustees had formulated a new policy that, if adopted, could rule out from school libraries books that were considered too controversial, including *Blood and Chocolate*. Under the new policy, the criteria for choosing library books would be favorable recommendations after examination by professional staff, the reputation of the author and publisher, and a broad and balanced representation of religious, ethnic, and cultural groups and issues.

As for *Blood and Chocolate*, it had been returned to the library shelves but placed on restrictive reserve, which meant a student would need parental permission to borrow it. "Because junior highs range in maturity levels, sometimes books are placed on restricted reserves," explained Chuck Davis, director of online learning at La Porte. After the final review of the new book policy, its ultimate fate would be decided.

Further Reading

Freedom Forum Web site. "School Systems across U.S. Challenge Books on Reading Lists," August 15, 2001. Available online: www.freedom forum.org/templates/document.asp?documentID=14624. Accessed October 25, 2007.

Houston Chronicle, July 26, 2001, This Week: 4; August 16, 2001, This Week: 1; October 4, 2001, This Week: 1; December 13, 2001, This Week: 1.

Smith, Cynthia Leitich. "Interview with Young Adult Book Author Annette Curtis Klause." Cynthia Leitich Smith Web site, December 2001. Available online: www.cynthialeitichsmith.com/lit_resources/ authors/interviews/AnnetteCurtisKlause.html. Accessed November 28, 2007.

About the Author of *Blood and Chocolate*

Annette Curtis Klause (1953–   )

Annette Curtis Klause is a leading writer of supernatural romantic novels for young adults. She attributes her interest in horror fiction to listening to her father tell her the plotlines of old horror movies when she was a young girl. Born on June 20, 1953, in Bristol, England, Klause moved to the United States as a teenager and earned a bachelor's degree in English literature from the University of Maryland, College Park. She went on to earn a master's degree in library science at College Park and supported herself as a librarian. From 1982 to 1994, she regularly wrote book reviews for *School Library Journal.*

Klause's first supernatural novel for young adults, *The Silver Kiss*, appeared in 1990. It is about a sixteen-year-old girl who falls in love with a vampire who is out to avenge the three-centuries-old murder of his mother. *Blood and Chocolate*, her third novel, was published in 1997. Her most recent novel is *Freaks: Alive, on the Inside!* (2006), the tale of a seventeen-year-old boy who joins a freak show in 1899 America.

Klause continues to work full time as a librarian and is head of children's services at the Aspen Hill Library in Maryland. She lives in Hyattsville, Maryland, with her husband and six cats. "I write so that I can be kissed by a vampire, travel to the stars, turn into a werewolf, and still be home for dinner," Klause once said.

The *Captain Underpants* Books (1997–   )
by Dav Pilkey

What Happens in the *Captain Underpants* Books

George Beard and Harold Hutchins are two mischievous fourth-graders who are always getting into trouble at Jerome Horwitz Elementary School. Their nemesis is their mean, ill-tempered principal, Mr. Krupp. One day the two boys hypnotize Mr. Krupp with their 3-D Hypno-Ring and convince him that he is not an elementary school principal but an outrageous superhero, Captain Underpants. The joke gets out of hand when, clad in his underpants, Krupp sets off to fight crime like any comic-book superhero. After accidentally drinking some Super Power Juice, the caped crusader really does develop the ability to fly. The boys learn that by snapping their fingers they can turn Mr. Krupp into Captain Underpants, and by throwing water on Captain Underpants they can instantly transform him back into Mr. Krupp.

Beginning with *The Adventures of Captain Underpants* (1997), George and Harold and their homemade superhero experience one outrageous adventure after another. In the first book, Captain Underpants does battle with the evil Dr. Diaper. In *Captain Underpants and the Attack of the Talking Toilets* (1999), the boys must stop an army of teacher-eating toilets. In *Captain Underpants and the Invasion of the Incredibly Naughty Cafeteria Ladies from Outer Space* (1999), aliens posing as cafeteria ladies turn students and teachers into zombie nerds. The evil Professor Poopypants shrinks the school and its occupants to miniatures in *Captain Underpants and the Perilous Plot of Professor Poopypants* (2000). A mean teacher is transformed into a super villain in *Captain Underpants and the Wrath of the Wicked*

Wedgie Woman (2001). In the two-part *Captain Underpants and the Big, Bad Battle of the Bionic Booger Boy* (2003), the school nerd tries to turn himself into a bionic superboy. In *Captain Underpants and the Preposterous Plight of the Purple Potty People* (2006), George and Harold enter an alternate universe controlled by their evil twins and a villainous Captain Blunderpants.

As of 2008, there have been ten *Captain Underpants* books, two *Captain Underpants Extra-Crunchy Book o' Fun* books, and two spin-off *Super Diaper Baby* books.

Challenges and Censorship

An abundance of gross-out humor and a complete disdain for adult authority, whether it be in school or at home, has helped to make the *Captain Underpants* series a publishing phenomenon for readers in elementary school. More than three million copies of the first book, *The Adventures of Captain Underpants*, were in print as of 2006. The subsequent titles in the series have all sold well. This same gross-out humor, however, has also lifted the Dav Pilkey books to eighth place on the American Library Association's "10 Most Frequently Challenged Books of 2005." The series ranked sixth in 2002 and fourth in 2004.

Central to the school challenges are the books' frequent references to poopies, pee pee, farts, wedgies, boogers, and various undergarments, including diapers, boxer shorts, and, of course, underpants. Another main reason for the challenges are the books' depiction of teachers and other authority figures as mean and stupid.

Pilkey's dislike for teachers comes from personal experience. In second grade, his attention deficient disorder (ADD) so frustrated his teacher that she put his desk in the hallway to keep him from disrupting the class. While sitting in the hallway, he told one interviewer, he began to create the Captain Underpants character in cartoon form. The same teacher tried to discourage Pilkey's drawing talents by tearing up one of his comics. "[She] told me I'd better grow up, because I couldn't spend the rest of my days making silly books," he said.

The adult Pilkey is not above poking fun at nearly everything, including libraries and the crusade against book banning. In *Cap-*

tain Underpants and the Preposterous Plight of the Purple Potty People*, George and Harold, the two unruly protagonists, enter the school library, where the librarian tells them, "This is Banned Books Week. Would you like to expand your minds today?" George replies, "Ummm . . . no thanks." The librarian is holding a copy of *Mommy Has Two Heathers*, a joke on the much challenged children's book about lesbian parents, *Heather Has Two Mommies*.

Pilkey's humor has won him probably as many adult fans as young ones, which may explain why many challenges are vehemently protested by parents of schoolchildren. Even those parents who aren't crazy about the books' content are pleased to see their children reading. "Sometimes I have parents who kind of go, 'Ewwww, Captain Underpants,'" said children's librarian Jane Bradkin. "They're not thrilled . . . but they know their kids love them and their kids read them."

One of these parents is author Denise Hamilton, who admitted in an article for the *Los Angeles Times*, "I'm never going to laugh as uproariously as my kids, but I've come around to thinking the books are pretty grossly funny. Besides, any book that teaches a five-year-old the meaning of 'perilous' and 'preposterous' is OK by me."

But perhaps the best defense for *Captain Underpants* comes from eight-year-old David Johnson of Naperville, Illinois, who told one newspaper reporter, "These books are really great if you like inappropriate humor."

Landmark Challenge:
Bad Role Models in Naugatuck, Connecticut

It wasn't the bathroom humor of *Captain Underpants and the Perilous Plot of Professor Poopypants* that most disturbed an elementary school principal and her superintendent in Naugatuck, Connecticut, in 2000, but it was the corrosive effect of the characters' antisocial behavior on fourth-grade boys.

The book was not in the library of the Maple Hill School, but it was brought in by a student from home. Principal Rebecca Sciacca was bothered by a chart in the book that encouraged readers to substitute bathroom-naughty names for their own by using the first letter of their real names. Thus, for example, Susan Anne Smith would become Snotty Diaper Fanny. Playing this game could result in name calling and hurt feelings, according to the principal, and she told the student to leave the book at home.

"The book was beginning to take on a life of its own," claimed school superintendent Alice Carolan, who supported Sciacca's actions but refused to condemn the series. "Just as we wouldn't have a subscription to *Mad* magazine in the school library," said Carolan. "There's nothing wrong with it. It's just not appropriate for school."

But for a number of parents, the *Captain Underpants* books were exactly the kind of literature that got students who were previously uninterested in reading to read. "We believe that one person should not have the sole discretion to decide which books should be banned from school libraries," said Dorothy Hoff, one of thirty parents who signed a protest petition and submitted it to the local school board. "And every parent that's read it, loves it."

Landmark Challenge: Super Diaper Baby and Deputy Doo-Doo Triumphant

"My gut reaction is that I don't like this book," said Betsy Schmechel, secondary education specialist in English and language arts in the Riverside, California, school district. But the freedom to read as out-lined in the First Amendment to the U.S. Constitution led Schmechel and five members of the district school board to reject a challenge to ban *Super Diaper Baby*, a spin-off book from the *Captain Underpants* series, in June 2003.

The challenge had been made by Pam Santi, guardian of her sec-ond-grade grandson, who read the book at John F. Kennedy Elemen-tary School. She decided something was wrong when she saw the second-grader drawing a picture of the book's villain, Deputy Doo-Doo. "A lot of parents and teachers have no clue what's in this book," she complained, calling it "inappropriate."

At their meeting to decide the issue, the board heard from one parent who supported the book. "This is a First Amendment issue," said Greg Taber. He argued that if Santi found the book offensive, she should steer her grandson to other books. "But don't take the right away from other children to read the book," he said.

The final vote was 5 to 2 in favor of keeping the book in the school library. Linda Wallis, a board member and second-grade teacher, cast one of the two dissenting votes. "There is not one teacher I know who wants [*Super Diaper Baby*] out there," she said. "This is not the type of humor we promote at school. It's putting down kids to say this is what they like to read." Sue Tavaglione, the other "no" vote, thought the book should be available only in a public library. "But it should not be in a school library," she insisted.

District librarian Christine Allen disagreed. "Not all books need to be morally uplifting," she said.

Further Reading

Carvajal, Doreen. "Keeping World Safe for Comfy Underwear." *New York Times*, April 10, 2000: C.19. Available online: http://query.nytimes.com/gst/fullpage.html?res=9E04EEDE163EF933A25757C0A9669C8B63&sec=&spon=&partner=permalink&exprod=permalink. Accessed December 7, 2007.

Chang, Elizabeth. "An Open-and-Shut Case: Captain Underpants and the Battle of Banned Books." *Washington Post*, September 28, 2005: C.11. Available online: www.washingtonpost.com/wp-dyn/content/article/2005/09/27/AR2005092701514.html. Accessed December 7, 2007.

Dav Pilkey's Extra-Crunchy Website o' Fun. Available online: www.pilkey.com. Accessed December 7, 2007.

Foerstel, Herbert N. *Banned in the U.S.A.: A Reference Guide to Book Censorship in Schools and Public Libraries*. Westport, Conn.: Greenwood Press, 2002.

Hamilton, Denise. "Just Hold Your Nose and Read: Sometimes You Gotta Do What You Gotta Do to Get Kids into Books." *Los Angeles Times*, August 11, 2006: B.13.

Megan, Kathleen. "A Kick For Captain Underpants." *Hartford Courant*, February 14, 2000: D.1.

Sauerwein, Kristina. "Super Diaper Baby Survives: A Riverside School's Committee Rejects a Request to Ban the Toilet-Humor Tome." *Los Angeles Times*, June 13, 2003: B1. Available online: http://articles.latimes.com/2003/jun/13/local/me-diaper13. Accessed December 7, 2007.

Zammarelli, Chris. "Truth, Justice, and All That Is Pre-Shrunk and Cottony." Bookslut.com, August 2004. Available online: www.bookslut.com/banned_bookslut/2004_08_002969.php. Accessed December 7, 2007.

About the Author of the *Captain Underpants* Books

Dav Pilkey (1966–)

David "Dav" Pilkey was born on March 4, 1966, in Cleveland, Ohio. A poor student in elementary school, Pilkey suffered from ADD. Later, while attending Kent State University in Ohio, a professor saw his comic drawings and encouraged him to try his hand at illustrating children's books.

Pilkey entered his first illustrated book, *World War Won*, in a national competition for student authors in 1987 and won in his age category. The book was published that same year. More books infused by Pilkey's outrageous sense of humor and childlike drawings followed, including *The Paperboy* (1996), which won a Caldecott Honor citation. The following year he published the first of the enormously successful *Captain Underpants* books. Other series from Pilkey's prolific pen include the *Dragon* books (1991–93), the *Creature Feature* books (1993), the *Dumb Bunnies* books (1994–97), the *Ricky Ricotta* books (2000–), and the *Big Dog and Little Dog* books (1997–2003).

Dav Pilkey got his nickname from an early job at Pizza Hut, where someone misspelled his first name on his name tag. He lives with his wife, Sayuri, three dogs, and a cat in Oregon.

APPENDIX 1

The American Library Association's "100 Most Frequently Challenged Books of 1990–2000"

(Books and authors in **boldface** are included in the **Our Freedom to Read** series.)

 1. ***Scary Stories* series, by Alvin Schwartz**
 2. *Daddy's Roommate,* by Michael Willhoite
 3. *I Know Why the Caged Bird Sings,* by Maya Angelou
 4. ***The Chocolate War,* by Robert Cormier**
 5. ***The Adventures of Huckleberry Finn,* by Mark Twain**
 6. ***Of Mice and Men,* by John Steinbeck**
 7. ***Harry Potter* series, by J. K. Rowling**
 8. ***Forever,* by Judy Blume**
 9. *Bridge to Terabithia,* by Katherine Paterson
10. ***Alice* series, by Phyllis Reynolds Naylor**
11. *Heather Has Two Mommies,* by Leslea Newman
12. ***My Brother Sam Is Dead,* by James Lincoln Collier and Christopher Collier**
13. ***The Catcher in the Rye,* by J. D. Salinger**
14. ***The Giver,* by Lois Lowry**
15. *It's Perfectly Normal,* by Robie Harris
16. ***Goosebumps* series**, by R. L. Stine
17. ***A Day No Pigs Would Die***, by Robert Newton Peck
18. *The Color Purple,* by Alice Walker
19. *Sex,* by Madonna
20. *Earth's Children* series, by Jean M. Auel

21. ***The Great Gilly Hopkins,* by Katherine Paterson**
22. ***A Wrinkle in Time,* by Madeleine L'Engle**
23. ***Go Ask Alice,* by Anonymous**
24. ***Fallen Angels,* by Walter Dean Myers**
25. ***In the Night Kitchen,* by Maurice Sendak**
26. ***The Stupids* series, by Harry Allard**
27. ***The Witches,* by Roald Dahl**
28. *The New Joy of Gay Sex,* by Charles Silverstein
29. *Anastasia Krupnik* series, by Lois Lowry
30. ***The Goats,* by Brock Cole**
31. *Kaffir Boy,* by Mark Mathabane
32. ***Blubber,* by Judy Blume**
33. ***Killing Mr. Griffin,* by Lois Duncan**
34. ***Halloween ABC,* by Eve Merriam**
35. ***We All Fall Down,* by Robert Cormier**
36. *Final Exit,* by Derek Humphry
37. *The Handmaid's Tale,* by Margaret Atwood
38. ***Julie of the Wolves,* by Jean Craighead George**
39. ***The Bluest Eye,* by Toni Morrison**
40. *What's Happening to My Body? Book for Girls,* by Lynda Madaras
41. ***To Kill a Mockingbird,* by Harper Lee**
42. *Beloved,* by Toni Morrison
43. ***The Outsiders,* by S. E. Hinton**
44. ***The Pigman,* by Paul Zindel**
45. *Bumps in the Night,* by Harry Allard
46. ***Deenie,* by Judy Blume**
47. *Flowers for Algernon,* by Daniel Keyes
48. ***Annie on My Mind,* by Nancy Garden**
49. *The Boy Who Lost His Face,* by Louis Sachar
50. *Cross Your Fingers, Spit in Your Hat,* by Alvin Schwartz
51. ***A Light in the Attic,* by Shel Silverstein**
52. ***Brave New World,* by Aldous Huxley**
53. *Sleeping Beauty Trilogy,* by A. N. Roquelaure (Anne Rice)
54. *Asking About Sex and Growing Up,* by Joanna Cole
55. ***Cujo,* by Stephen King**
56. ***James and the Giant Peach,* by Roald Dahl**
57. *The Anarchist Cookbook,* by William Powell
58. *Boys and Sex,* by Wardell Pomeroy

59. *Ordinary People,* by Judith Guest

60. *American Psycho,* by Bret Easton Ellis

61. *What's Happening to My Body? Book for Boys,* by Lynda Madaras

62. *Are You There God? It's Me, Margaret,* by Judy Blume

63. *Crazy Lady,* by Jane Conly

64. **Athletic Shorts, by Chris Crutcher**

65. *Fade,* by Robert Cormier

66. *Guess What?,* by Mem Fox

67. *The House of Spirits,* by Isabel Allende

68. *The Face on the Milk Carton,* by Caroline Cooney

69. *Slaughterhouse-Five,* by Kurt Vonnegut

70. *Lord of the Flies,* by William Golding

71. *Native Son,* by Richard Wright

72. *Women on Top: How Real Life Has Changed Women's Sexual Fantasies,* by Nancy Friday

73. **Curses, Hexes & Spells, by Daniel Cohen**

74. **Jack, by A.M. Homes**

75. *Bless Me, Ultima,* by Rudolfo A. Anaya

76. *Where Did I Come From?,* by Peter Mayle

77. *Carrie,* by Stephen King

78. *Tiger Eyes,* by Judy Blume

79. *On My Honor,* by Marion Dane Bauer

80. *Arizona Kid,* by Ron Koertge

81. *Family Secrets,* by Norma Klein

82. *Mommy Laid an Egg,* by Babette Cole

83. *The Dead Zone,* by Stephen King

84. **The Adventures of Tom Sawyer, by Mark Twain**

85. *Song of Solomon,* by Toni Morrison

86. *Always Running,* by Luis Rodriguez

87. *Private Parts,* by Howard Stern

88. *Where's Waldo?,* by Martin Hanford

89. **Summer of My German Soldier, by Bette Greene**

90. **Little Black Sambo, by Helen Bannerman**

91. *Pillars of the Earth,* by Ken Follett

92. *Running Loose,* by Chris Crutcher

93. *Sex Education,* by Jenny Davis

94. **The Drowning of Stephan Jones, by Bette Greene**

95. *Girls and Sex,* by Wardell Pomeroy

APPENDIX 2

The American Library Association's "10 Most Frequently Challenged Books of 2006" and the Reasons for the Challenges

(Books and authors in **boldface** are included in the **Our Freedom to Read** series.)

1. *And Tango Makes Three,* by Justin Richardson and Peter Parnell, for homosexuality, anti-family content, and being unsuited to age group
2. *Gossip Girls* series, by Cecily Von Ziegesar, for homosexuality, sexual content, drugs, being unsuited to age group, and offensive language
3. ***Alice* series, by Phyllis Reynolds Naylor,** for sexual content and offensive language
4. ***The Earth, My Butt, and Other Big Round Things,* by Carolyn Mackler,** for sexual content, anti-family content, offensive language, and being unsuited to age group
5. ***The Bluest Eye,* by Toni Morrison,** for sexual content, offensive language, and being unsuited to age group
6. ***Scary Stories* series, by Alvin Schwartz,** for occultism/Satanism, being unsuited to age group, violence, and insensitivity
7. ***Athletic Shorts,* by Chris Crutcher,** for homosexuality and offensive language
8. ***The Perks of Being a Wallflower,* by Stephen Chbosky,** for homosexuality, sexual content, offensive language, and being unsuited to age group

9. *Beloved,* by Toni Morrison, for offensive language, sexual content, and being unsuited to age group
10. ***The Chocolate War,* by Robert Cormier,** for sexual content, offensive language, and violence

APPENDIX 3

The American Library Association's "10 Most Frequently Challenged Books of 2007" and the Reasons for the Challenges

(Books and authors in **boldface** are included in the **Our Freedom to Read** series.)

1. *And Tango Makes Three,* by Justin Richardson and Peter Parnell, for anti-ethnic content, sexism, homosexuality, anti-family content, its religious viewpoint, and being unsuited to age group
2. ***The Chocolate War,* by Robert Cormier,** for sexual content, offensive language, and violence
3. *Olive's Ocean,* by Kevin Henkes, for sexual content and offensive language
4. ***The Golden Compass,* by Philip Pullman,** for its religious viewpoint
5. ***The Adventures of Huckleberry Finn,* by Mark Twain,** for racism
6. *The Color Purple,* by Alice Walker, for homosexuality, sexual content, offensive language, and being unsuited to age group
7. *TTYL,* by Lauren Myracle, for sexual content, offensive language, and being unsuited to age group
8. *I Know Why the Caged Bird Sings,* by Maya Angelou, for sexual content
9. *It's Perfectly Normal,* by Robie Harris, for sexual content
10. ***The Perks of Being a Wallflower,* by Stephen Chbosky,** for homosexuality, sexual content, offensive language, and being unsuited to age group

APPENDIX 4

Web sites on Book Censorship and Challenges

American Booksellers Foundation for Free Expression
www.abffe.org

This site is useful for its Banned Books Week Handbook, which includes many interesting features such as "Stories Behind the Bans and Challenges."

American Library Association
www.ala.org

The official website of the ALA has a wealth of information on challenged and banned books, including yearly lists of the top challenged books and archives for the ALA's Newsletter on Intellectual Freedom.

National Coalition Against Censorship
www.ncac.org

This site includes updated news on censorship issues, including Supreme Court decisions. There is information on censorship of not only books, but also art, music, science, and entertainment.

APPENDIX 5

Banned Books Week

Early each fall, the American Library Association (ALA) sponsors Banned Books Week nationwide. It is an opportunity for everyone who loves to read—and cherishes the freedom to do so—to draw attention to that precious right. The first Banned Books Week was celebrated in 1981.

Here are some ways the ALA's Office for Intellectual Freedom suggests you can celebrate Banned Books Week:

1. Read a banned book. Look for a favorite or something you've never read before on the book lists in Appendix 1, 2, and 3. You might choose one of the books discussed in this volume.
2. Talk about the First Amendment in school. Make it the focus of a class discussion. The First Amendment to the U.S. Constitution reads: "Congress shall make no law respecting an establishment of religion, or prohibiting the free exercise thereof; or abridging the freedom of speech, or of the press; or of the people peaceably to assemble, and to petition the Government for a redress of grievances."
3. Organize your own Banned Books Read-Out! at your school, a public library, or local bookstore. Invite a local author, banned or otherwise, to read from his or her work. Have adults and children read selections from banned books.
4. Join the Intellectual Freedom Action Network, a grassroots group of volunteers who are willing to come forward in defense of the freedom to read in censorship controversies in your school or community.

5. Join another organization that advocates intellectual freedom, such as the Freedom to Read Foundation.
6. Write or call your government representatives in Washington, D.C., and let them know you want them, in their role as legislators, to protect your freedom to read.

If you have your own ideas for how to celebrated Banned Books Week, e-mail them to the Office for Intellectual Freedom at oif@ala.org. They'd be happy to hear from you!

INDEX